Just Another Elysian Sidetrip

By

Sirena West

ISBN: 1-4107-8099-6 (e-book)
ISBN: 1-4107-8098-8 (Paperback)

Library of Congress Control Number: 2003110581

This book is printed on acid free paper.

Printed in the United States of America
Bloomington, IN

1stBooks - rev. 09/19/03

For my husband and children
And for those who shared their own elysian
sidetrips with me

Chapter one:

The Realm Begins

Fade-in.

It took jumping off a ship, stealing an airplane, and even some extreme mountain climbing; but in the end, as any well-respected film aficionado knows, the dashing Robert Conway, portrayed by an equally dashing Ronald Colman, rediscovers his Shangri-La in Frank Capra's classic, *Lost Horizon*.

Pity, Mr. Conway didn't have Tasha Felding as his travel guide. Oh, he would have had to still jump off a ship and all, but with her in the driver seat, he would have had a lot more fun, not to mention sex. If there was ever a person with the divine gift of stumbling, tripping, or backstepping into some erotic Elysian journey, vacation, excursion, or even a short sidetrip, it was one Natasha Marie Goldberg Felding. And anyone within her realm of that moment of stumbling, well, they just needed to hold on for the ride, as her three college roommates Elizabeth, Dawn, and Miranda quickly discovered.

It all began so innocently in September, 1969, after a summer of love and Woodstock, when Tasha arrived at Parnassus Canyon University in Topanga, California, totally pissed off at the world, and her father. She had specifically requested only coed dorms and here she was waving her little dorm confirmation card that stated *Tudor Hall 407*, an all-female dorm. No amount of persuasion on her mother's part could convince Tasha that her own father didn't pay off some high ranking university official.

"You know you're quite lucky," the overly perky resident assistant at the front door said, "Tudor has traditionally housed the *creme de la creme* of PCU women, so there is status and some perks to being one of the only four freshmen in this dorm."

"Which are?" Tasha asked sarcastically.

"Well you will already be at the top of the list for a room next year and by your senior, if not junior year; you could definitely have your single with private bath."

As if Tasha wouldn't end up where she wanted by her senior year anyway.

"Oh fuck," Tasha muttered as she stepped into the tiny room, totally shocked that this day could get even worse.

"Yes, it will require some creativity if we going to enjoy any breathing space."

Tasha immediately turned around to see who the hell this Mary Poppins was, and almost lost her breath, "Oh god," she hissed, "or should I say goddess?"

Tasha had just come face to face with the first of her three roommates: the living, breathing incarnation of Grace Kelly, if not Hera, herself. 5'5", slender, tan, classic features, natural blonde hair, sea blue eyes, and legs that should be required to carry a license. Shit, it was going to be a long year. "Best All Around?"

The beautiful young woman smiled and nodded.

"Homecoming Queen?"

She smiled and nodded again.

"Scholastic award winner and maybe school politics?"

The blonde smiled even bigger and nodded.

"Fuck," Tasha said as she turned away and ventured on over to the window.

"You're not used to competition, are you?" the goddess said smugly.

"No. And I don't feel like starting now," Tasha growled.

"Well neither am I. But something tells me we're going to rule over different segments of the campus," she said in an obvious attempt to be friendly, which Tasha only found condescending. "By the way, my name is Elizabeth. Elizabeth Adams..."

Tasha immediately turned to look at her, and let out a rather cruel haunting laugh. It apparently unnerved Elizabeth a bit.

"Yes, I'm WASP. Episcopalian even."

"Wealthy?"

"Well."

"Old money?"

"Yes, but I don't want to rely on that."

"Well, I would ask you why you are here and not at some sister school, but I'm hoping to transfer to a coed dorm this week, so I don't see the need to bond."

"Funny.   I can't help but think that any dorm in which you reside automatically becomes coed," Elizabeth said crossing her arms.

"Calling me a slut?"

"Yes.   But I mean it as a compliment."

The irony was Tasha believed she did mean it as a compliment.

"Hi, I believe this is 407?"   a woman said standing outside the door.

"What? The four, the zero, and the seven on the door gave it away?" Tasha blurted out.

"I'll be sure to put you on the welcoming committee when I'm president of this school," Elizabeth said sarcastically to Tasha before addressing the new roommate.   "Hi, my name is Elizabeth."

"I'm Dawn Wolfe, from Arizona."

"Nice to meet you, I read your essay in the newsletter. You deserved the Walter Tudor scholarship."

"Fuck," Tasha muttered under her breath as she checked out the latest goddess to enter the realm: A stunning Navajo women, who stood a lean 5'6" and had high cheekbones and silky, long straight hair that Tasha could only dream of. But her biggest draw were her emerald green eyes that sparkled against her dark skin. Obviously there had been an outsider in her family tree somewhere.

"Most Likely to Succeed?" Tasha said, more stating a fact than as a question.

"What?" Dawn asked.

"Nothing, she's just a little obsessed with high school accomplishments," Elizabeth said before turning to taunt Tasha. "And now we have Athena in our midst."

"As long as I'm Aphrodite," Tasha shot back.

"I guess that makes me Eris, the goddess of discord, but you can call me Miranda." another young woman announced as she pushed into the room, and took her rightful place smack dab in the center.

"Shit," Tasha blurted out. This latest and hopefully final addition was 5'7", had short auburn hair and a supertoned body. "Most Athletic?" Tasha said.

"Of course. I'm here on a combined athletic/journalism scholarship. And, just to add to your misery, I was on the campaign trail with Robert Kennedy and even attended the Democratic Convention. My interviews with some of the demonstrators were published in newspapers all over the country which won me the Michigan State High School Journalism Award."

Tasha wanted to crap. Elizabeth called it right. Tasha was not use to competition. No matter the time or place, she shined, it was that simple. Granted, she was not traditionally pretty, with small eyes, chipmunk cheeks, wide lips, and unruly dark hair; but, if anyone knew how to take individual pieces to produce one sexy image, it this little goddess. Even during the mod days of straight hair, Tasha kept her hair loose and curly, knowing that it conjured up images of her just getting out of a bed. And granted, she only grew to 5'4" and had inherited full-figure genes, but her years of dance training kept her from being plump. As one summer theatre director said, "There's a difference between being attractive and being hot. And Tasha, you're hot!"

"So, you were voted..." Elizabeth asked.

"You're going to hate me," Tasha smiled.

"Probably, but let's get it out in the open."

"Biggest Flirt."

"God, I knew it. You're right, I hate you," Elizabeth said, only half-joking.

"I hate you, too, does that me we can't share a closet?" Tasha surprised herself with this statement. After all, she was planning on transferring.

"I thought you were going to request a transfer?" Elizabeth said in a manner that suggested Tasha either joined them now or get out.

"Based on what complaint? I've been assigned to a room full of goddesses?" Tasha surprised herself even more. Here she was basically committing herself to this room, to the realm of goddesses. But then, where else should a hot goddess be?

"Okay, goddesses," Elizabeth commanded, "Let's start unpacking and Tasha gets a top bunk, because who knows how many nights she will actually sleep here." Miranda and Dawn immediately shot a look of disgust over at Elizabeth. "It's okay. I mean it as a compliment." They then quickly looked at Tasha with apologetic looks on their faces.

"It's okay. She does mean it as a compliment." Then she smiled slyly, "Besides she's right."

"Well since I'm assuming you're not going to add much to our collective GPA, I propose we three claim the study desks first, and you get what's left," Miranda suggested.

"I'll take a top bunk, if I can have the desk with the best lighting," Dawn jumped in.

"I'll need the corner, since I'm left-handed," Miranda said.

"Actually, I was hoping for that one..." Elizabeth started.

"Shit," Tasha muttered, "you coeds are actually here for some serious studying. Crap, if I get in your way, or get too close to your turf, just call in Officer Krupke."

The other three just looked at her, totally lost.

"Was that a non-sequiter?" Miranda asked.

"Sorry. A little *West Side Story* humor. You know, fighting over your turf in this ridiculously small room." Tasha felt stupid, first about the joke, and then the attempt to explain it; but was vindicated when Elizabeth began snapping her fingers, followed by the other two, and then Tasha herself joined in. This kinetic sound never did create harmony between the Jets and the Sharks, but it did wonders for these four young women, who were laughing hysterically within seconds.

"Okay, let's get it out in the open. I would be a Jet," Elizabeth said.

"Oh yeah. Like your mom would ever let you get near some high-school drop out or rebel without a cause," teased Tasha.

"Excuse me. I think you and I had the same upbringing. Just different prayers. Besides, I don't see the wild one waiting outside for you."

"*The Wild One*. I'm impressed. Good Brando classic. What are you rebelling against?"

"What you got?" they both chorused breaking into even more hysterics.

"So confess," Tasha continued her teasing. "Did you sneak out with Penelope or Muffy to see it?"

"I watched it at home."

"Parents in Europe?"

Elizabeth grinded her teeth, "Yes," she said softly.

"Nanny asleep?" Tasha continued.

Elizabeth growled, "Yes!"

"Doesn't count," Tasha announced victoriously.

"What do you mean? Do I have to provide proof that my escorts to the debutante ball were named Loser and Blue?"

"Wow! Now I am impressed. *Wild Angles*. You had to have seen that at the theater?"

"Yes. And I did sneak out. With Priscilla."

"Fellow debutante?" Tasha asked.

"Yes. And don't even think that doesn't count."

"Au contraire, my queen goddess, you actually earned extra points here."

Tasha turned to unpack and noticed a beautiful rag doll on Dawn's bed.

"Well, if I can't sleep with some gorgeous freshman football player, can I sleep with her?" Tasha teased.

"Nice try. But this doll is mine. Her name is Glipsa. Made for me by my Aunt Amy. She is the Navajo goddess of education and knowledge."

"Wow, even the dolls in this room are goddesses," Tasha said in resignation.

"See, you do belong here," Dawn said sincerely.

"You know, I think I do," Tasha said in a rare moment of seriousness. Then in her best Betty Davis impression, stated, "Fasten your seatbelts. It's going to be a bumpy ride."

"That's what we're counting on," Elizabeth smiled.

Later that night, after all the orientations, the four returned and pulled out their night clothes, and to no one's surprise, distinct styles emerged.

"No offense, Tasha, but isn't that wasted on us?" Miranda asked regarding the red satin nightgown complete with décolletage.

"Panty raid?" Tasha offered.

"I don't think so," Miranda answered. "Oh, but you would have competition with this," she said pointing to Elizabeth in an ivory color silk camisole and shorts ensemble.

"Well we know who the scholarship students are in this room," Miranda said as she and Dawn dressed in their two piece flannel set and oversized t-shirt respectively.

Elizabeth asked firmly, almost demanding, "Don't make such statements."

Miranda shrugged, "Why? We all know how we got here. What's the big deal?"

"I don't think how we got here should be the focus, but rather what we do here," Elizabeth offered.

Even Tasha wanted to throw up on that note.

"Face it," Miranda said to Elizabeth, crossing her arms and standing tall, "You'll always be the rich prom queen." Miranda said to Elizabeth.

Not to be outdone, Elizabeth stood just as tall, "And you'll always be the champion of the underdog, which means you'll blend in as much as I will"

Tasha, who was sick of all this posturing, jumped in, "And Dawn will most likely be the quiet, studious, but mystical one.

"And you, what?" Miranda asked.

"I'm afraid to know," Elizabeth said sitting down.

"Well, let me give you a hint," Tasha said as she pulled out a plastic sweater bag. "You heathens may have had your doubts. But I did make the acquaintance of some motorcycle hood this summer."

"The pizza delivery guy on a scooter doesn't count, Tasha," Elizabeth said.

"Oh, ye of little faith. Let me present you this." She pulled out the cashmere sweater and unfolded it. Inside was a well-worn vest covered with a gang-related insignia.

Elizabeth snarled, "So you met some obese unwashed slob. I could do that."

"You Philistines. He was a rebel with a sensitive soul, and intelligence that was too complex and deep to cope with the mindless conformity of mainstream society."

"He sure delivered a lot with his pizza," Miranda giggled, causing Elizabeth to almost choke on her laugher.

"And this, too." Tasha then pulled out a nickel bag of marijuana and some zig zags. "Care to join me. In his memory."

Dawn and Miranda looked at one another and paled. It was obvious to Tasha that neither had tried it before.

"What a surprise," Elizabeth waved a hand in a half circle. "I'm in, but only on the condition that we do it in the bathroom down the hall," she again waved her hand, ordering her troops to follow. "Just promise us your friend won't be making too many visits to our hall of academia," Elizabeth said, as she sat on the heater at the end of the bathroom.

"I thought college was the place to expand your horizons," Tasha said as she down on the toilet, getting the joints ready.

"Not to mention our minds," Miranda sat on the tub, with Dawn seated next to her on the floor, her long dark legs extended.

They were about to light up, when they heard the voice of Sheri, the Resident Assistant. Tasha quickly grabbed the bag of dope and threw it to Elizabeth who threw it into a built-in linen closet.

"Oh good, you're still up. Wow, am I entering a party or something?" asked Sheri.

"Just the realm of the goddess. Goddesses of 407," Tasha answered.

"I'm impressed. This hellhole has never looked so warm and homey," Sheri said.

"Our powers are infinite," Tasha said.

"They must be. Well, as I was saying, it's a tradition to get a picture of everyone's first night in the dorm. I was going to take it in the room, but, you all look so comfortable and at home."

"It's our realm," Elizabeth said.

"So, everyone smile and say sex," Sheri said.

When Sheri left, Elizabeth opened the cabinet and proclaimed the dope missing.

"It can't be." Tasha bitched.

"Wait...wait. Just a minute. Wow. This is fun," Elizabeth said.

"What is. What's in there? Some Hell's Angel or something? Tasha asked.

"I suspect you'll find this almost as good, knowing what little I already do about you. Look. There's a fake back to this cabinet. I threw the dope in with such force I guess, that it knocked the back sideways a little and slid way the hell back there."

The other three walked over and looked inside.

"That is so neat. One of you with long arms, can you reach in and grab it?" Tasha looked at Dawn and Miranda. "This is truly our realm. I mean we even have been given a perfect place to stash the dope."

"You're not serious about keeping it in here, are you?" asked Miranda.

"Well, what else will it be good for?"

"Maybe secret files from secret sources," Miranda answered.

"Oh, please, Lois Lane, just how many exclusives are planning on your freshman year?"

"Many.   But I doubt that they'll equal the number of your one night stands."

"Goddesses!" Elizabeth yelled.   "Now stop this.   First of all, if Tasha is going to have dope, well, better here than in our actual room.   And if you want to use it also, Miranda, go ahead.   Personally, I just thought it was funny, and I'll probably never look at it again.   How about you Dawn?"

Dawn frowned and crossed her arms.   "I don't know.   Me think I will draw a Kokopelli on wall and let future anthropologists write a thesis on it."

Elizabeth tossed her hands in the air. "Fuck it, you all do what you want with it. Good night."

"Elizabeth, I'm sorry."   Dawn dropped her stance.   "Don't run off because of me."

"Actually, Dawn," Tasha said, "I think the cave drawing idea is great.   I think we should do it, and leave some stupid riddle or something too.   And," Tasha's imagination was starting to build, "and, we can leave an address or phone number for any person who comes across the riddle and can answer it."

"That is so stupid and such a waste of time, I love it. I'm in," announced Elizabeth.

With felt tip markers, the four drew a picture of Kokopelli, the famed little flute-playing character found on rocks and in caves throughout the southwest, and asked the question, who were the four goddesses of 407.

"What do they get if they answer correctly?" Miranda asked.

"We'll pay for their textbooks for one semester. Be sure to include that in note," Tasha instructed. "Now can I light up?"

The four instinctively sat in their original seats and lit up a joint.

By the time the joint was making its second round, it was decided that Elizabeth would run for class president.

"Okay. Now for you three. I mean, I want company at the top. No mere nymphs, no offense, Tasha."

"None taken."

"If we're goddesses, then we all need to find our little kingdoms, or as Tasha puts it, our realms."

Miranda was the first to jump in. "This past summer, I hung out with some of the women who were elected officers for the Associated Women Students. They said they would help me campaign if I wanted to be the freshman rep, and I do. Their agenda this year includes dropping the damn tea parties and the bridal fashion shows and work on more significant issues for women." She then laughed heartily. "I'm afraid I'm not going to be one of the glowing beautiful goddesses who stands around and creates pretty music. I'm going to create some major discord."

"That's fine. Homer would not have had anything to write about without some conflicts," Elizabeth said. "How about you, Dawn?"

"I don't know. I think Glipsa will have to stand in for me. I'm not really goddess material."

"You know, Dawn," Miranda interrupted, "They have a great Minority Student Council on campus. It monitors discrimination and harassment, plus assists with loans and scholarships. It also provides academic tutoring and career counseling. They'll be looking for a freshman rep."

"Well, I'm sure there are other qualified freshmen."

"But none will be from the goddess zone," Elizabeth laughed.

"Okay, you can promote me. But I'm not much of a campaigner."

"Good. Three down, one to go. Miranda, what do you have for Tasha?" Elizabeth asked.

"I'm a goddess. Not a miracle worker," Miranda half smiled.

"Sweet, you two. But, I'll have you know that I've actually been recruited for something."

"Dear, god!" Miranda moaned.

"Come on, Miranda, give her a break. I mean, even Gloria Steinem was a Playboy Bunny. What could be more demeaning that that?"

"Cheerleading," Tasha announced.

"Oh, Christ, except that," moaned Elizabeth.

Everyone booed and hissed for a few moments, before Tasha defended her choice as a chance to enhance her dancing and choreographing skills.

"Well," teased Miranda. "We better see some innovative routines out there. Something worthy of Martha Graham."

"I don't know if the school colors are black, but I will do my best," she promised. "So, are you snooty, intellectual goddess okay with my choice of kingdom?"

"Actually, I'm somewhat relieved. I thought for a minute, your whole purpose would be to snag some cute freshman football player," Elizabeth confessed.

"Honey, that's not a purpose. That's a given."

"Pretty confident. I mean, granted, we're goddesses and all, but there are some knockouts out there. Didn't you see them at all the orientation meetings?" Elizabeth asked.

"Mere mortals."

"Shall we expect company tonight. Or will you be snagging him at his place?" teased Elizabeth.

"Oh his place. And not tonight. Tonight I give myself to you. But don't get used to it," Tasha laughed.

"Okay," Elizabeth egged her on, "So when does this big snag take place?"

"By this weekend," Tasha nodded.

"I don't believe this," complained Miranda, "for a moment, I thought we were here for a higher purpose. Now we're talking about bedding a jock."

"I'm surprised, Miranda, by your cynicism. I mean your are the one true jock of this group," Tasha pointed out.

"Jock. Not the jock groupie. Big difference."

"Well, we all have our talents," Tasha said. "Tell you what, goddesses, if I don't snag one by this weekend, I will buckle down, and place myself on probation until I achieve a 3.5 GPA," Tasha offered.

"Wow, you are confident," Elizabeth said.

"But, if I do succeed, then my first term paper, compliments of you three."

"That's unethical," Miranda scolded.

"Well, I tried. How about my laundry for a month?"

"I'm in," Elizabeth said. "And it has to be a bona fide date. Not a one night stand with some horny guy who prays his steady girlfriend doesn't find out."

"Oh, ye of little faith."

Thus, that late evening, the realm of the goddesses was born. While the physical surroundings were small, the realm, in spirit, was large enough to encompass and nurture four strong distinct personalities. Each would grow even stronger and more distinct with each passing day: The regal Elizabeth, the turbulent Miranda, the halcyonic Dawn, and last, but never least, the mercurial Tasha. There was never a misunderstanding, a bruised ego, or an out and out fight that was strong enough to break down the walls of the realm, providing each goddess within, a sense of security and serenity, two essentials often needed in their hectic tenure at PCU.

Chapter two:

The Continuation of the Realm

Sheri must have found the picture of the four in their bathroom so endearing that she had a poster made from the negative and posted it on the bathroom door. "*Entering the realm of the goddesses,*" was printed on the bottom. She also turned in the negative to the yearbook editor, who chose it for the title page of the freshman section.

What Sheri did not know, though, was that almost every Thursday, the goddesses would enter their realm, and pass around a joint, while discussing philosophy, life, and most of all, their busy schedules.

For the goddesses of 407, success came quickly. Within a few weeks, all could write home and inform their families that they had achieved their first goals, although Tasha left out the bit about snagging the cute football player that first weekend.

Tasha went ahead and allowed her roommates to be impressed by her conquest, but she recognized immediately that cute Phillip Connely, quarterback of the freshmen team, was now bored with his high school sweetheart, Eileen; and all she had to do was emit some vibes, and wait for his hormones to complete the task. For the first part of that year, Tasha and Phillip were the envied couple, quarterback and head cheerleader, a little too cute for Miranda, but as the goddesses had agreed, there would be different purposes to their existence on campus.

It all became even cuter when Tasha was nominated for the Homecoming Court, but alas, she would lose to class president, Elizabeth P. Adams. Tasha did bounce back, though, when she was the only freshman to be cast in school's production of The *Fantasitcks,* portraying the Mute to critical success. She also won the heart of the senior male lead, Don Shidell, and during the run of the show, they were the darling couple of the Theatre Arts department. For years Tasha would brag that when she dropped Phillip, he made the rebound with not a cheerleader, but with other theatre arts major.

"And that means what?" Miranda had asked.

"That he grew during his tenure with me."

Miranda never quite understood that logic, but then there was a lot about Tasha, on which she would never get a handle.

Elizabeth, who reigned beautifully during the homecoming game, was escorted that evening by an old, but not so dear friend, Kip Morgan, the handsome wide receiver of the freshmen team, and the son of the president of the Board of Trustees, John Morgan. Kip pursued Elizabeth from the start of their freshman year, but Elizabeth had not been raised to be anyone's trophy, so Kip, eventually set his eyes elsewhere.

And it was where he set them that surprised everyone. The recipient of his well-crafted charm was fellow Pschye 101 student, Dawn Wolfe. What was even more surprising was that Dawn was receptive.

"Just one question, Dawn," Elizabeth asked one evening as they passed around the joint. "What the hell are you thinking?"

"I'm with Elizabeth on this, Dawn," Tasha chimed in. "I mean, he's even superficial for my taste, and that says a lot. There are so many other cute jock types out there, and I know a bunch that are totally intrigued by you and think you're exotic."

"Yeah, they think I can whip up rain in a second," she laughed. "By the way, did I tell you? We're going out to dinner this weekend. In his Porsche?"

"I think I'm going to be sick," Miranda lamented. "Tasha, I can see. But I had higher hopes for you, Dawn."

"I love and respect you, Miranda, but it's not your place to dream my dreams," Dawn firmly reminded her.

"I know, but, I need to say this. Doesn't the fact that he started dating you around mid-terms tell you something?" Miranda said.

"Yes. He's using me to get help on his homework."

"And that doesn't bother you?"

"A little."

"Well," Miranda was on a roll, "Do you get anything out this? And please don't tell me, love and affection, because no matter what he is saying to you at night, he does not mean it."

"Mellow out, Miranda. I know what a cad he is. I know he's only dating me for my homework and because it's somewhat trendy for boys like him to date a minority at some point. Let's face it; I'm quite possibly his only rebellious act."

"And he is your, what?" Elizabeth asked.

"My one and only opportunity to know my father."

The three just looked at her.

"Come on. I told you a million times. I was conceived when my mother was gang-raped by a bunch of white guys. And obviously it was the sperm of the one with green eyes that won the race."

"I still don't get it, Dawn," Miranda said.

"Kip has blue eyes. My father has green eyes. Other than that, I figure they're cut from the same cloth."

"Isn't this a little out of Oedipus?" Tasha asked.

"Don't worry, dear, I haven't slept with him, and probably won't. But this may be the one and only opportunity to get to know the kind of man that could produce someone like me—the illegitimate daughter of a Navajo rape victim."

Not much silenced this crowd, but that comment did. From then on, the other three never questioned her relationship with Kip, until one Thursday night before winter break, Dawn asked her roomies if anyone was free for a movie or something that weekend.

"You're not seeing Kip this weekend?" Miranda asked.

"Not unless I bump into him somewhere. And you know what?"

"What?"

"I wasn't deprived at all growing up without my father."

"Did he hurt you?" Tasha wanted to know.

"No," Dawn smiled, "He may be an arrogant brat, but I don't think he would actually hurt anyone."

For reasons she couldn't explain, Tasha wasn't so sure of that.

Kip did not fade from their lives though. Miranda quickly made a name for herself on campus as both a radical feminist and a ruthless and relentless reporter with a liberal bent. However, her articles did infuriate some conservative administrators, Board members, and even a few students. Some continuously complained about her position on the paper, but no one did it as often as Kip Morgan. When the paper paid Miranda's airfare to interview students at Kent State, Kip not only wrote in defending the presence and actions of the National Guard, but questioned why a scholarship student should be flying around the country at the school's expense when she was not contributing anything financially to the institution.

"My interview was reprinted in I don't know how many papers and was nominated for a major college journalism award, not to mention the recognition it gave to both the paper and school.   And this pompous oaf questions my contribution to this school?" Miranda bitched in the bathroom as they passed around the joint.

"I mean I don't mind having a sparing partner, but I would like someone a little more worthy, a legitimate foe.   Not some shallow, stupid puppet for the board.   I know he would never debate me live, because he couldn't think on his feet."

"You're right," Tasha nodded and took her hit, "it's a known fact at Olympia Hall that John Morgan calls Kip and dictates his letters over phone.   Sometimes his latest girlfriend types them up and sends them to the paper."

"I swear I never did," Dawn added.

"You know, Miranda," Tasha said, "you're the only one who takes his letters seriously. You shouldn't let them get to you."

"I can't be like you.   I can't ignore legitimate problems."

Tasha would had been insulted, but she had long ago accepted the fact that Miranda considered her the most shallow of the group and respected her opinions the least; so Tasha let that comment, plus many more, go.

In May, when it came time to select roommates and rooms for the next year, the four shocked the head residents and almost everyone else on campus when they opted to stay together in 407. Sure, they could remain a group in a larger nicer suite, but somehow over the year, 407 had truly become their realm.

Their sophomore year turned out to be just as eventful. Elizabeth served as Commissioner of Activities and met her community service requirement by becoming a reading tutor for inner city kids.

Miranda was once again an ace reporter, V.P. of the Associated Women Students, top middle-distance runner, and performed her required community service by working the hotlines at a teen center.

Dawn also kept busy as secretary for the Minority Student Council, and worked at the same teen center as Miranda.

Tasha performed to standing ovations as Anne Frank in *The Diary of Anne Frank*, and outgrew the cheerleading squad. Unlike the others, did not do her community service project, but instead completed her internship, with a newly formed politically-inclined theatre company, known as the Kaleidoscope Company. Needless to say, within months, she was involved with one of the founders, Jacob Felding.

Tasha and Elizabeth were both nominated for the homecoming court again and consoled each when they both lost. They shared the honors a second time by both being nominated for the Winter Solstice Festive, with Elizabeth once again being the victor. That spring, however, Tasha finally had her day, when she was the sophomore princess for the Mayfest Festival.

At the end of the year, they again upset the apple cart, when they elected to remain a group in 407 for their junior year.

During their junior year, Elizabeth was ASB vice president and interned in a free legal clinic, where she became convinced the law was her calling.

Tasha was named lead choreographer for the dance ensemble; wowed audiences as the new wife in *Desire Under the Elms*; and completed her community service requirement by teaching dance and acting classes at a government-subsidized after school center, where many of her friends from the *Kaleidoscope Company* also taught.

Dawn kept busy as board member of the Minority Students Council, but also functioned as V.P of Phi Beta Kappa on campus, which included Elizabeth and Miranda as members, and interned at a shelter for runaway teenagers.

Miranda, once again, was star reporter, track star, campus feminist, and interned as a publicist for a rape clinic, which to her surprise, serviced many PCU women. She shared this surprise with her fellow AWS members and together they proposed, for the following year, a year long rape and sex crime awareness project, which was approved, thanks to the efforts and persuasive talents of Elizabeth. Elizabeth also used her clout to get Miranda named as one of the committee organizing members.

Socially, they held their own, as Tasha and Elizabeth continued with their tradition of being nominated for the homecoming court, and winter solstice, although neither made the final cut. They began to worry about losing their touch, but regained their confidence, when during the spring's *Festival of Dionysia*, Tasha wowed them the lead in *Lysistrata*, and was crowned Aphrodite. The biggest surprise and thrill, though, was the election of Dawn as one of the nine Muses to sit on Tasha's court.

This outstanding year, however, was marred by the sudden heart attack death of Jackson Taylor, Miranda's father, right before the winter break. Miranda did not return to school until a week after second semester had started and it was quite apparent that something inside her had died along with her father. Her patience and tolerance of others, especially those she considered politically naive or stupid was now almost non-existent and she basically refrained from any small talk or social exchange. Her presence in the weekly Thursday night bathroom sessions was rare, which did not upset her roommates too much, as her tongue had become quite biting and critical.

By the end of the year, three of the goddesses of 407 had begun wondering if it was time to relinquish 407 and move on to singles as was their divine rights. Assuming that Miranda was equally as sick of them as they were of her, they brought it up gently one evening, only to find her breaking down in a rain of tears. It took Dawn, the psychology major, to figure out that Miranda had already lost so much, that she didn't need to lose any more, so she volunteered to remain with Miranda, and the other two followed. Each prayed that the summer would ease her pain and theirs.

Summer did not ease her pain, however, and Miranda returned just as cynical and critical, but with the hectic schedules the four kept, the atmosphere in 407 remained copasetic.

Elizabeth served as president of ASB and finally wore that homecoming crown. Tasha continued as the diva of the theatre department and acquired an agent who landed a few commercial spots for her. Dawn remained active in Phi Beta Kappa and Minority Student Council and was the recipient of the psychology fellowship, which looked great on grad school applications, but also meant she spent a lot of time grading Psyche 101 papers and exams. Miranda receives a fellowship and course credit as one of the directors of the rape aware program and continued with reporting and track.

As the year progressed into second semester, the sense of closure began to take place. Elizabeth was accepted at all the law schools at which she applied, but settled on Stanford. Tasha was accepted in a New Jersey Theatre Repertory Company, which was not too far from Broadway, or a certain director from the Kaleidoscope Company. Dawn, who had enjoyed her stay in California, announced she would be returning to Arizona to pursue her PhD in psychology at University of Arizona in Tucson. And to no one's surprise, Miranda was accepted at the Columbia School of Journalism.

"One journey ends. Another journey begins," Tasha said one Thursday night passing around the joint.

Sadly, only three of the journeys would stay on course. One would take a drastic detour.

Chapter three:

One Not So Elysian Detour

"Hello." Tasha said, so thankful for the phone call, no matter whom it was.

"Hello, movie star."

"Hello, Kip," nobody else used that moniker with her. "So, surprised I actually reached you. I thought you would be blowing that mid-term off and be at Pete's by now. He said referring to the sleazy, cheap rock and roll dive that was home to every senior and lower classmen with fake ID (about half the PCU population) on Tuesdays. But on this particular Tuesday evening, March 10, 1973, Pete's was going to have to do without Tasha, and the rest of the goddesses of 407.

Elizabeth was swamped with ASB work and was basically living in her office for a few days. Dawn was at her office, grading Psyche 101 papers. Miranda was in Bakersfield, or was it Barstow, conducting interviews with members of the United Farm Workers. And Tasha was uncharacteristically practicing self-discipline by staying home and trying to make some sense of RNA and DNA and other letters from the Biology 101 text for a mid-term the following morning. Of course, every other senior had taken that course long ago, but somehow Tasha was convinced that the general ed requirements would be modified just for her convenience or that she would be given a lead in a movie, forcing her to drop out of college. But, alas, the fates decreed no such order, and now Tasha was stuck taking this miserable class, surrounded by a bunch of 18 year olds. The one perk, of course, was that there were plenty of young men who did her lab reports for her, but for the mid-term—she was on her own—and out of dope, too.

"I told you the other day, I have no choice, I must pass this class," she reminded him.

"Well, movie star, I can help."

"Oh shit," she said with major mixed emotions. Kip had a history of helping her and other selected pretty women on campus, but, of course, it always came with a price. Tasha had to determine what she could afford.

"Oh come on, movie star, when have I let you down or let any cats out of the bag. You know I always take care of my favorite clients."

"Honey, at the moment I don't need dope—well actually I do, but what I really need are the answers to a certain fucking Bio 101 mid-term."

"Got both. And both are yours for the price of one," he said smugly.

"What do you mean?"

"Simple. I got a bag of great dope here, usual price, and because you're one of my favorite customers, I will also hand you over the copy of tomorrow's mid-term, complete with answers."

"How did you?"

"Let's just say, the store is open and another one of my favorite clients is a T.A. in the Bio department, and he just couldn't come up with the cash. So we bartered."

"Oh Kip, I owe you!"

"Yeah, you do. Just get your ass down by the bleachers at the practice field within the next hour. Ricky and Larry are picking me up there for Pete's."

"Well, hon, couldn't you just drop everything by on the way to Pete's?"

"Do I look like some fucking pizza guy? Get your sweet ass down there, or stay straight and flunk the test." Then he hung up.

"Ah, shit." She was totally out of cash and that meant she was going to have to borrow some money from Elizabeth to pay him. Well, not even borrow—hell, it was not her fault that Mr. Adams was more generous that her own father, and if Elizabeth hadn't learned by now not to keep large sums of cash in what she thought was a secret place, well...

"Fuck!" Tasha screamed.

"What are you up to, Tasha, or do I even want to know?" asked Miranda who stormed into

42

the room, bitching about the farm workers who stood her up for the interview. Tasha remained quiet, as Miranda tore off her Lois Lane togs, changed into her running outfit, and bolted out the door to run off her built up anger.

Feeling a bit unnerved by that intrusion, Tasha reached into Elizabeth's suitcase and grabbed all the bills and stuffed them in an envelope. Hell, she would return the majority of the money later. And she was going to have to borrow Dawn's car again. Without her knowledge again. But then it wasn't fair that Dawn's uncle was more generous than her own father, and if Dawn hadn't learned by now not leave her keys in what she thought was a secret place..."

"So, the doctor's little girl is going to flunk her one and only science class," Kip laughed as he passed the joint to Tasha, but kept hold of the exam.

"Don't be such a Philistine, Kip. You know if I don't pass, my father will either kill me or have another heart attack, if not both," Tasha laughed as she leaned back against the old bleacher and inhaled.

"But come on, cutie, your folks must be immune by now. I mean, what have you ever done to make them proud?" Kip was not only getting loaded but already had his share of alcohol in his system.

"You shit." Tasha teased as she socked him playfully in his arm. "And what about you, Mr. Son of President of the Board of Trustees. How proud would your father be if he knew that you were the biggest dealer on campus?"

"He would appreciate my entrepreneurship."

"Yeah sure," Tasha laughed taking another hit.

"Yes. But I'm even more sure that you were appreciative of my father intervening when that stupid head resident busted you and all those freaky theatre arts majors for drugs your sophomore year."

"No doubt," Tasha blew smoke in his face.

"I mean, your ass could have been expelled just like all those others freaks.

Especially that bitch, what was her name again?"

"Nancy," Tasha answered, knowing where this conversation was going, but was too loaded to fight it.

"And wasn't Nancy the lead in *Anne Frank* and your biggest rival in general?"

"Yes, Kip she was, and yes, her expulsion allowed me to get the lead and almost every lead after that.   And yes, my father never even heard about the famous theatre department drug bust.

"Thanks to..."

"You and your father," she repeated for him.   "Shit, Kip, how many times are going to bring that up."

Kip leaned over and kissed her.   "As often as I can."

"Philistine," she muttered in between a few kisses, not really sure if that comment was for him or herself.

"You know, Tasha, you still have the distinction of..."

"I know, Kip, I know.   Being the one and only woman you and your father have shared."

"My daddy still thanks me. Although, he was hoping I could have brought him Elizabeth and Dawn, too. But those two fucking saints never got into trouble."

"How about Miranda? Wasn't she always in trouble with you guys?" Tasha joked.

"That dyke. Hate that bitch. Never could understand why you three beauties kept her around."

"Kip, I'm going to tell you something that you're not going to understand. But we love her."

"Oh gross," he said as he began to fondle her breasts. "Do you love like this?"

Tasha continued to smoke the joint, allowing Kip in his drunken/loaded stupor, to clumsily play with her bosom. With a semi-serious relationship with Jacob Felding, a promising and influential off-Broadway director, and a host of other older, more mature men on her resume, the silliness and immaturity of the likes of Kip Morgan now bored her. But here she was anyway, all because she could not face studying for a Biology mid-term. As she inhaled once again, she made a vow that this would be the last time she would ever rely on Kip Morgan or any of his buddies for anything.

"Kip, I need to get comfortable," she said as she pushed him away a bit.

"Yeah, you do. You know why? Cuz you're going to get fucked again. Fucked by your favorite, Kip Morgan...hey wait. Be quiet."

"What?" Tasha asked, right before Kip placed his hand over her mouth.

"This could be my night. Or hers."

Tasha struggled, but Kip held her tight. "You stay here and if you're good, you can show me how exactly you love the dyke."

Tasha hadn't a clue what he was talking about until she saw Miranda running their way.

"Oh shit," she muttered. Nothing good could come out of this.

"Hey dyke, you need a finger in you? Hey, Butch, is this where you meet all your lesbo lovers?"

Tasha rolled her eyes and wondered if Kip was ever going to grow up.

"Hey, Lessie, uh, hey, gonna get some ass?"

While still safely hidden in the dark, Tasha could see Kip step out of the shadows, obviously inebriated, and stagger over to Miranda.

"Hey, dyke. Why don't you try some real loving for a change? With a real man."

Miranda kept her cool and tried running around him.

"Come on baby. Give me some pussy. No one will have to know. None of your dyke friends. Come on, it's just me and you here," he taunted to Miranda jumping all around, blocking her path.

Tasha was about to step out and remind him, that it was actually the three of them there, when he began reaching for Miranda. She backed away, trying to avoid an ugly confrontation.

"Just go away, Kip. Let me run now," she said in a very soothing voice, with a hint of fear.

"Hey, low-class, needy scholarship dyke, I am Kip Morgan. Who the hell are you to tell me what to do?

"Please, Kip, just go away," Miranda said, with a little more fear creeping into her voice as she walked backwards around the bleachers as he pursued her. When he lunged at her, she jumped a good three or four feet away and screamed that he was a bastard.

"Oh no, now, you called me a name. Not a very nice name. You need to learn a lesson. You need that as much as you need a good fuck. And I'm here to give you both." Tasha for sure was going to run in and make him back off, but when Kip pulled out a switchblade and began twirling it, like some "B" movie character, Tasha froze.

"Come on, dyke, be a good girl, and Kip will make you smile. Come to Kip," he said, already headed toward her. Tasha was now trying to figure out a way to effectively disarm him, when he took a swipe at Miranda, barely missing her torso.

"Kip, you're fucking drunk. You're being an idiot. Go away," Miranda yelled.

"No, Kip no go away. Kip stay here and fuck your brains out. Now come here, you bitch." He lunged the knife at her, but Miranda swiftly jumped out of his way each and every time, until she found herself trapped against the bleachers. Quickly thinking, she hopped onto the first bench and then ran up until she reached to top, about twenty feet off the ground. She looked down and saw that Kip, in his drunken state, was following her up. With nowhere to go, she jumped down and land safely.

Kip reached the top, and presented himself to the world, with his right foot on the top railing and arms stretched out. "Hey, I'm Pepe LePew, going after..."

His upper body wobbled, causing his right foot to slip off, and over the top he went.

For Tasha, it was all in slow motion. As Kip tumbled forward, his left pants leg got caught on a piece of loose wood, breaking a six inch chunk of it off, as it remained stuck in the pants. On the way down, his right arm first went out and then came back in, with the blade upright, positioned directly underneath his chest. When contact with the ground was made, the thump came loud and clear, as his body bounced about an inch once before staying put on the ground, with the blade inside his chest, and his head exploding from coming face to face with a rock about the size of a cantaloupe.

Except for her heart beating ferociously, and some runaway urine, Tasha was numb with shock. When she finally regained control of her large motor skills, she delicately approached Miranda who was now standing by the body and also in a complete state of shock, so much, that she wasn't even surprised by Tasha's appearance.

"Well, we were wrong along," Tasha said. "He did have brains. Hell, a whole lot of them." And the two of them broke out into hysterical laughter, before looking at each other and realizing what just had transpired. Their laughter immediately turned to tears.

"Holy, fucking, shit," Miranda sobbed.

"It's okay," Tasha said placing an arm around her. "Listen, you stay here, I am going to go back to Tudor and get Betsy to call the police. I'll be back as soon as possible. Now don't touch a thing."

"I'm not waiting with no fucking dead body."

"Okay. You don't have to," Tasha said somewhat surprised by her lack of cooperation. "I'll wait here and you go to Tudor. Here, I have Dawn's keys; her car is over there on the side street."

"I can't go back to the dorm and I definitely can't call the police."

"Well, then who will call the police?" Tasha asked somewhat irritated through the tears.

"Beats me. But it can't be us."

"Miranda, what are you talking about? We need to report this accident, we witnessed it."

"Accident? Accident?" Miranda yelled.

"Yes, accident. What do you want to call it?" Tasha yelled even louder.

"I call it an accident. You call it an accident. But do you think for one minute our distinguished President of the Board of Trustees will call it an accident and do you think our distinguished Sheriff Department of Topanga will call it an accident?" Miranda sobbed, as she crossed her arms over her chest. "I don't think they'll call it an accident. I think they will call it murder."

"That's ridiculous."

"Is it? Wealthy, powerful John Morgan is going to allow his son's obit read that the drunken fool fell on his knife after fucking the school's slut and trying to fuck the school's radical."

Wow, those words stung, but Tasha knew there were more pressing issues.

"Miranda, I may be the school slut and you're the school radical, but we're not murderers."

"No one will believe us, you poor fool," Miranda yelled.

"Why not? Look at the evidence. Shit, you never even touched the knife, there will be no fingerprints. And that piece of bleacher sticking out of his leg, oooh, god, looking at his body, makes me sick." Tasha quickly turned away, afraid she was going to lose dinner.

"The hell with the physical evidence. That can be lost or altered. Remember me; I'm the one who did the investigative piece of the Topanga Sheriff's Department, especially their handling of young liberal suspects. The piece that now has them in hot water."

"Oh, your timing does suck," Tasha agreed.

"Perfect payback for them. And for John Morgan too. Oh yes, I can see the obit now.

His All-American kid with wholesome traditional value was butchered by that radical trouble-making feminist with some axes to grind."

"But, you still have me. I am a witness."

"And they'll claim other witnesses, too. Witnesses we never heard of. Witnesses too well-rehearsed that even your star power can't match."

"But I am a true witness."

"Tasha."

"And I am a doctor's daughter."

"You're."

"A product of private education," Tasha said raising her voice.

"You're a."

"A volunteer in the community. A teacher of dance to underprivileged kids." she said even louder.

"Yes, you're a."

"Plus, I am the only bona fide witness," she practically screamed, trying to get through to Miranda.

"You're a slut!" Miranda countered, so loud that it actually echoed. "A lying, cheating, fucking slut."

Tasha felt the whole world come to a sudden stop as those words slammed her in the face. She knew Miranda never held her in high regard, but this commentary of her lifestyle seemed a bit out of place, not to mention vicious.

"Listen, I am not passing judgment. But don't you see, you'll be easy pickings for the prosecution."

"No, I don't see."

"Tasha, come on, your ability to look into a friend's eyes and swear you've never slept with her boyfriend, while he is sneaking out the back door is legendary. And everyone knows you have had at least ten grandparents die in order to postpone mid-terms or finals. Not to mention all those papers you really never wrote."

"Enough!" Tasha screamed. She began to shake and cry even more.

"Not to mention, your drug bust."

"What? Tasha screeched.

"And the fact that you fucked father and son to escape expulsion"

"How the fuck do you know? I mean who all knows?"

"Don't worry. Not too many people. But Tasha, see what I mean? I know a lot about deals and cover ups. Morgan and his people are not good people, but they are powerful. And they can hurt us both. For sure, they will pin this murder on me and fabricate the evidence to convict me. They will do the same to you, or blackmail you into lying, or if by some strange chance, you insist on doing the right thing for a change, and testify on my behalf, my god, they could crucify you on your freshman year alone. Tasha, I'm afraid you are the worst possible witness I could have now," she said, through a flood of tears and a sense of hopelessness.

Tasha knew she was right. It would take no effort to discredit her, thus validating some phony story, whatever it would be, by default. For the first time that she could remember, she actually felt some remorse and some guilt about her behavior. Here her roommate was in serious trouble and she was now a liability more than anything.

"What are we going to do?" Tasha whispered through the tears.

"I suggest you go back to the dorm and claim to know nothing. That's the only way you will be safe. I'm taking a hike. I don't know where, but I better get started." Tears flowed freely again.

"That's not good enough, Miranda."

"What?"

"For better or worse, you got stuck with me in this mess. Granted, you would be better off with Elizabeth or Dawn, but the fucking fates gave you me. Now what are we going to do?" Tasha made it clear that neither one of them was going to move without some sort of plan in place.

Miranda stood there for a second. "I don't know. I'm scared," she said still sobbing.

Tasha was dumbfounded. She had never seen Miranda cry before, much less scared and ill-prepared to handle a situation. Tasha reached out and placed her arms around Miranda's muscular body and guided her to a sitting position. "You know, Miranda, nobody knows about this but us. We can just leave, and act surprised along with everyone else when the news hits the campus. Let's both go back to the dorm and pretend we were there all night."

"I don't know. I've never been as devious as you," Miranda said in her tears.

"Thank you," Tasha said, knowing there was no compliment in there at all.

"But, Tasha, you must promise me one thing. I know it's hard for you to keep promises, but this is the one time in your life you must."

"What is it?"

"No matter what. Even if I get my ass dragged in jail. Do not let on that you were here or you know anything. And I say that because I'm investigating a case right now that involves our new best friends, Morgan Sr. and Topanga's finest, and one sweet witness who could have provided an alibi for the defendant. Right before she was to testify, she had a fatal drug overdose. Funny, nobody ever knew her to use drugs prior to that."

"Miranda, are you suggesting?"

"Plus, you really could be a better use to me if you function as a liaison between me and the Marlborough Man."

"Who?"

"He's a great source. You can trust him. But no one else. Got it?"

"Yes."

"Promise me you will only communicate with him but even then, you won't do anything until I give the word. Promise," Miranda demanded.

"Yes, for sure I do promise. Now I'm getting the creeps here. So let's go and you can give me details back in the room. Come on, goddess, let's go back to the dorm." Tasha helped her taller roommate up, dropping Dawn's keys and the envelope of Elizabeth's money.

"Listen pick those up, I better go check and make sure I didn't leave an earring or something," she although her main concerns were the dope and the test. After she wandered over into the shadows, she turned and noticed that her stunned roommate had wandered over toward the main road, where her silhouette could be seen by a passing car. She was about to holler at her, when all of sudden, a car piloted by Kip's friend, Ricky, drove up and she could hear Ricky yelling some derogatory remark to Miranda who all of sudden awoke from her coma and began running in the other direction.

"Oh shit," Tasha muttered softly as she instinctively moved off the field and onto a well-hidden fire trial.

"Hey, Kip, are you there? Where the fuck is you?" Larry, a passenger in the car, yelled.

"He ain't going to answer you, schmuck," Tasha whispered to herself as she carefully took another step back.

"Hey, Kip, hey. What the fuck! Kip! You okay. Hey, bitch? Why are you running? Jesus, fuck!" Ricky screamed.

Tasha saw them get out of the car and attempt to run after Miranda, which under other circumstances would have been comical as she was naturally the better runner, and they were completely drunk. At this point, Tasha realized that Miranda had Dawn's keys and was running toward the car, and that Ricky and his friend, Larry were now running toward Kip's body. Tasha quickly stepped back deeper into the shadows and increased her pace. She could barely see them still, as they approached the dead body.

At that point, she then felt safe enough to turn and actually run back to the campus.

If the fates had been cruel earlier that evening, they were now in a more cooperative spirit, as there was no one in sight as Tasha entered the side door and ran up the back stairs to the study hall. She could hear voices on the floor and decided her best bet would be to sit in the study hall until someone came looking for her. And she knew they would.

Chapter four:

Finishing the Realm

Time may fly if you're having fun, but if you're waiting to give the performance of a lifetime—that is, convincing everyone from roommates to college presidents and Topanga sheriffs that you are totally surprised by the sudden death of one of your classmates, well time can drag. And did it ever drag, especially since it wasn't until 11:30 before anyone came looking for Tasha.

"Hey, the light is on in the study hall, she might be in there" said Dr. Luther, President of PCU.

"Tasha? You're kidding right?" said Betsy, the Head Resident.

"Philistines," Tasha muttered to herself as she waited for them to come in and confirm that it was indeed her in the study hall.

"Tasha, you are here," said Betsy obviously surprised.

"Yes, I have a killer mid-term tomorrow," although Tasha knew that all classes would be canceled the next day.

"Listen, Tasha, President Luther and I need to speak with you. And with Elizabeth and Dawn, too. In fact, they should be here shortly."

Then right on cue, Elizabeth and Dawn were escorted in by Casey Baker, head of PCU security, and members of the Topanga Canyon Sheriff's Department, headed by Detective Anthony Degas.

Tasha shot a look at Elizabeth stating, "What the hell did you do?" and Elizabeth responded with a look that said, "Me? I thought it was you?" Before they could start shooting looks at Dawn, the president spoke.

"Ladies, I regret, I must present you with some bad news."

The three ladies instinctively joined hands and braced for the worse. "This evening," he continued, "the body of one of your favorite classmates, Kip Morgan, was found dead by the bleachers at the football practice field."

Whether Kip was one of their favorites or not was open to debate, but that matter seemed unimportant now. Elizabeth inquired as to what had happened, if they knew.

"It appears that this young man fell victim to foul play. He was apparently stabbed repeatedly."

Tasha kept her composure, but wanted to know when one self-inflicted stab wound equaled repeatedly stabbed.

"But, I regret to tell you that is not all the bad news I have for you." He paused and looked at them. All three of them remained silent. "I need to ask you. Do you know the presence of whereabouts of your other roommate, Miranda Taylor?"

"Yes," blurted out Elizabeth, "she's in Bakersfield..."

"Barstow," corrected Dawn.

"Thank you. She is interviewing farm workers for a piece for the paper."

All the adults looked at each other.

"President Luther."

"Yes, Elizabeth?"

"Why are you concerned about Miranda's whereabouts?"

"You see, Miss," Det. Degas jumped in, "we have two witnesses who have placed Miss Taylor at the scene of the crime at the time of the murder."

"But this is absurd. You know Miranda never advocated violence."

"I know this is hard for you three. And trust me, nobody wants to believe that Miranda is involved in any way," President Luther spoke. "But we must let the officers do their jobs. Now, they have warrants to search your room. I'm going to ask that you three to cooperate."

"Of course," Elizabeth said.

Just then, Tasha got a very sick feeling inside. Oh shit, she thought, how could she have been so fucking stupid? When the detectives entered the room, Tasha wanted to beat her own face in.

"What is this?" Det. Degas asked indicating Elizabeth's small suitcase.

"That belongs to me," Elizabeth answered obviously mortified to find in open and empty.

"Is there anything missing?" he asked.

"Yes," whined Elizabeth. "About five-hundred dollars."

"How about this?" the detective asked about Dawn's jewelry box.

"That's mine and I believe my car keys are missing," Dawn said in total disbelief.

"What is the make and color of your car?"

"A red Volkswagen beetle."

"Ladies, Miranda was seen leaving the crime scene in a red VW," Dr. Luther informed them.

Tasha knew it would be an eternity if not longer before she would stop kicking herself for not putting those things away. Poor Miranda, what else could she do to implicate her poor roommate in this tragedy.

"Plus," Dr. Luther continued, "we already checked the campus phone records. Kip apparently placed a call to this room earlier."

"Bingo," Tasha thought in total disbelief. Did the fates truly want Miranda's life ruined forever?

"And if you three weren't here as you claim, then Miranda must have been the one who spoke to him."

"But what does it all prove?" asked Elizabeth. "We've been roommates for four years; we sometimes borrow things and replace them. And who knows why Kip called here in the first place."

Betsy came over and placed her arms around Elizabeth. "Dear, I know this is hard for you, but the hard cold cruel realty is that Kip had heard something about his name being mentioned by Miranda in regards to a cheating scandal."

"Sounds like vintage Miranda to me. But not the killing part," Elizabeth said through tears.

"Maybe she was there, but she would never physically harm anyone," Dawn offered.

"Dear," Betsy said, "Kip's friends, Ricky Zogobo and Larry Davidson, had been waiting for him at Pete's. About ten o'clock, they became worried and went looking for him. They found him, alive, with Miranda at the practice field. The two of them were shouting at each other and when Kip started to walk away, he said something about exposing her stories as fraud, well she pulled out a knife and stabbed him, stabbed him in the chest." At this point, Betsy was in tears.

"It's just not adding up right," Elizabeth said.

Tasha could concur. She was no math whiz, but boy, the calculations were way off. First there was the issue of the time; Tasha seemed to remember Kip being dead by 8:30. Then there was the business about his brains splattered all over the ground, or the lack of mention of that aspect. Miranda was right. They did fabricate witnesses and a story. Tasha just now had to pray that neither Ricky nor Larry knew of her earlier rendezvous with Kip.

About this time, many of the fourth floor residents began returning home and the story of Kip's tragic demise and the alleged involvement of Miranda began to spread like wildfire, not just in Tudor, but all over the campus. Needless to say, very few students slept well that evening, partially due to the intensive manhunt for Miranda throughout the dorms and everywhere else possible.

Somewhere throughout this excitement, President Luther announced that classes would be canceled the next day, and he pulled Elizabeth aside and asked if she would address the student union in the morning, and urge them to remain calm and cooperative until this whole matter was resolved. Elizabeth agreed and then called her father, who, even in the middle of the night, listened to her ideas for her speech and promised to be there in the morning for support.

By the next morning, the campus was aflame with gossip and innuendoes, and to hold back the impending tide of anger that seemed to be building, the university held a press conference.

"According to our investigation," Degas told the crowd, "Kip was planning on meeting his two friends, Larry Davidson, and Ricky Zogobo, at a popular student hangout. Around 7:30, he called them and told them that he had received a phone call from Miranda Taylor, accusing him of being part of a cheating ring on campus. Even though, this was a ludicrous accusation, Kip agreed to meet with her later that evening. Later, when Kip had not joined his friends, they decided to go looking for him and they found him at the practice field. The two young men could hear Kip Morgan and Miranda Taylor arguing. Kip waved at them and told Miranda he had had enough, and started to walk toward the car. At that point Miranda pulled out a knife, grabbed Kip and stabbed him in the chest. She then continued to stab him many more times more before dropping him to the ground. The two witnesses, jumped out of the car, but Miranda took off running into the dark canyon. They stopped to try to help their friend, who was, unfortunately, already dead. And by that time, Miranda was out of sight. They then drove to another spot on campus and called John Morgan, father of the victim, who called us. We are in the midst of an all-out search for Miranda Taylor, but she is still at large. We consider her armed and dangerous. And we would like to remind everyone, that aiding and abetting a fugitive in a felony crime."

When Degas was finished, President Luther introduced John Morgan, who denounced the revolutionary thoughts and rhetoric of the New Left and proclaimed his son a martyr who was murdered for his traditional, pro-American values. He then announced a reward for any information that could lead the authorities to Miranda. He urged anyone who had information to be cooperative and help bring the vicious murderess to justice. "And, if any one of you, have your doubts regarding her guilt," he cried from the podium. "Think about this. We have the greatest and most fair justice system in the world. And she is on the run. As the ancient philosopher Syrus, once stated, *He who flees from trial confesses his guilt.*"

Ronald Adams hugged and kissed his daughter right before she stepped up to the podium. "My fellow students, for the last four years, I have felt blessed by the diverse nature of this wonderful, experimental university. The campus is comprised of students of different backgrounds, religions, cultures, and points-of-view. It is no secret, that my roommate, Miranda Taylor, and my childhood friend, Kip Morgan, represented two diametrically opposing points of view on almost every issue facing us on campus. Their constant letter exchange in the *Iliad* became as familiar as mid-terms and homecoming games. Yet their debates were always welcomed. On this campus, we have strived to make everyone feel welcome and to hear and respect all sides of an issue. I, like many others, sometimes agreed with Miranda Taylor. Sometimes with Kip Morgan. Maybe with one more than the other. But, like everyone else, I admired and respected these two people for willingly expressing their opinions and beliefs."

Elizabeth paused, took a breath.

"Knowing both parties as I do, I am deeply saddened by the death and the accusation. But I am also confident that neither party was of a violent nature. I thank President Luther and the Topanga Sheriff's Department for sharing with us what they know so far. But let us all remember, there are still a myriad of unanswered questions. We must resist jumping to conclusions, casting blame, and taking sides, we, as university students, are here to examine, explore and determine the truth about things. And during this time of trial, it is essentially important, that we heed some other words of the philosopher Syrus, who stated, *And we must hold out for the truth.*" Elizabeth then looked down at her father who was beaming with pride.

"I ask the student population, the faculty, the board of trustees, and everyone affiliated with PCU to extend their love and support to the families of Kip Morgan and Miranda Taylor. I ask that we all be grateful for the years that Kip graced out lives with his charm and school spirit, and I ask that Miranda Taylor please display trust in our legal system and come forth. Thank you."

"Well done," Dawn whispered to Elizabeth as she stepped off the podium.

"Thank you. But it wasn't enough to spare us. Ladies," she said softly to Tasha and Dawn, "I envision a couple of weeks ahead of us that will rival the Labors of Hercules."

How prophetic she was.

Miranda's reputation as an activist and the fact that she was suspected of crossing state lines, although Dawn's car was found only an hour away, allowed the FBI to become involved. And their quest for an alleged notebook full of names and phone numbers provided the incentive to question, nag, and even follow the three until Elizabeth's father exerted some clout and the agents backed off. That was then followed with meeting Miranda's mother, Rosemary Taylor, weakened from lung cancer. While they understood her distress and frustration, her wailing could easily rival any Greek tragedy heroine and her innuendoes that somehow they were part of the system out to destroy her daughter proved to be emotionally exhausting. They were even less successful in providing satisfactory answers for both the lawyers from the D.A. office and the ones retained by Rosemary.

"God, I never experience such dissatisfied audiences," moaned Tasha a few days later sitting in the bathroom.

"You know, it's not just the reporters, the lawyers, and all the students looking at us, as if we had the answers," Elizabeth added. "It's an awful feeling, sort of like an undertow, waiting underneath, just waiting, and waiting, for the perfect moment to pull me down. I have never felt so vulnerable in my life," Elizabeth explained.

"Me either," confessed Dawn. "We always joked about being invincible and having powers. But fuck, this is reality, and no title, or posters, or bathroom session is going to make it better."

Tasha really wanted to apologize at that point. After all, if she hadn't goofed off and put off taking Biology 101 until her second semester senior year, she wouldn't have been freaking out about the mid-term and she wouldn't have met Kip and maybe then Kip would not have seen Miranda running. Tasha shut eyes her eyes tight, trying to stop the tears.

"It's okay to cry, Tasha," Dawn sympathized. "We both know how you feel."

No they didn't. But until further notice, it was going to stay that way.

Chapter five:

Kip's Final Journey

The most awkward surreal moment came that Saturday when the three attended Kip's memorial service. Kip had been quickly cremated, because, according to the official story, the Morgans wanted everyone to remember Kip as his beautiful, vivacious self. Tasha suspected the fact that his head end up in a million pieces had something to do with it. Plus, with his body gone to ashes, it would be hard to refute the so called medical examiner report, which clearly stated that not only had

Kip died from multiple stab wounds but that his body was free from any alcohol or illegal substances. If Tasha didn't believe Miranda when she said Morgan was powerful, she believed her now.

"Shit," Tasha said as she felt a pair of strong hands take hold of her waist.

"Sorry, I didn't mean to scare you. I'm just so glad you are here. Your presence makes every place a little bit better, even my son's service," John Morgan said as he pulled her close into him. Tasha began to pray that no one was noticing. He then whispered in her ear, "Tasha, I'm sending Kip's mother to a resort in Colorado. It will do her a lot of good. She's leaving tomorrow morning. I want you to come by the house around 2 in the afternoon. And if you still have it, wear that gorgeous red dress. Here's some money for a cab." Morgan quickly stuffed the money in her hand and was gone.

"My god," she whispered to herself. "Does he know that I know?" Tasha thought. Tasha spent a good part of the service wondering what kind of deal she would be making with the devil. But later, when he again brushed her hair and quietly commented that he recalled she liked that, she guessed that Morgan was just some horny bastard taking advantage of a coed. Either way, she knew it would behoove to show up at the appointed hour in the appointed attire.

"Tasha you look stunning as ever," John Morgan said the next afternoon as he greeted her at the door.

"Thank you, Mr. Morgan," Tasha smiled as she entered entering the beautiful mansion with the ocean view.

"Ah, what did I tell you the last time? John. Please call me John."

"My pleasure, John."

He took her into his office. "See, Tasha. This is the desk I was sitting when I got that call from Kip a few years ago. That call when he told me a good friend of his had been in the wrong place at the wrong time and needed help."

"I will always appreciate your help, John," Tasha said sitting on his desk, and suggestively crossing her legs.

"Oh, my pleasure. After all, there are very few true stars in this world, much less on PCU's campus. I didn't want to lose the one we had," he said stroking her calves.

"Thank you."

"You know Tasha, I do believe in your talent. I've seen all the productions. You are star quality. But you know it takes more than talent and beauty, which you have plenty of. It takes some good breaks."

"You're right," Tasha said somewhat relieved that this was going to be a casting couch session as opposed to an interrogation.

"I have friends in the industry. I can get you so many auditions," he said leaning into her.

"How sweet of you. But you have done so much already." she said, fighting the urge to not fight him off.

"But I can do more," he said as he pulled her toward him. "Let me help you."

What Tasha noticed this time was that John Morgan did not give choices. He was going to help her whether she wanted him to or not. And no doubt, he would expect her to return the favor.

John began to kiss her, talking in between the wet lip-locks. "Sam Cannon is putting together a few new pilots and Tony Winters is creating a brand new soap opera. I can set up meetings," he said coming up for air.

"If you're okay with that. I don't want to take advantage," she said, trying to act as if she was really enjoying herself.

"Oh take advantage, please take advantage," he said touching her breasts.

Just then the phone rang and John yelled out a few cuss words before picking up the receiver. He began to tell the person he was busy, but it became apparent that he needed to finish this conversation.

"Tasha, honey, it's essential I take this call. Listen, there's a bottle of champagne in kitchen, and a few glasses. Could you go get them and meet me up in the bedroom? You remember where it is, don't you?"

Tasha nodded and did what she was told, but on her way to the stairs, she noticed the office door was not closed tightly, plus John's voice was rather loud. Carefully she stood by the door and listened.

"I don't care," John roared. "We lucked out that Schwartz, Mann, and Jenkins were not around that night. We just need to make sure they are kept busy enough that they don't have time to poke around in this case. Shit, I don't care. Create some crime to keep them busy. Shit, we've done it before. And no, don't worry about the boys. They were Kip's best friends and they loved him. Plus, Larry, he's from a poor family, and was on an athletic scholarship. He's easy to buy. Ricky? Shit, my favorite fool. Thinks he has enough charm to never have to have a real job. You know those Communication majors. Well, I just keep providing him with those jobs. I know, I know. Listen, we'll find that bitch sooner or later. In fact, I have some lovely company right now at the house that might just help me with that. In fact, I better go now. I've kept the lady waiting long enough."

Tasha then quietly sprinted up the stairs and was in the bedroom before Morgan even left his office.

Tasha was relieved that all John wanted out of her was the whereabouts of Miranda. Hell, she could create a false trail if needed. Like many others of her generation, Miranda had been weaned on the civil rights movement and the movie, *Easy Rider*. If Miranda has one area of bigotry, it was that she was scared of the south; so Tahsa figured that would be the one geographical area Miranda would avoid like the plague.

Later, after an afternoon of sex and champagne, John began inquiring about Miranda, her family and her friends. Tasha, who was not as drunk as she was playing, blabbed something about a PCU graduate who was an editor of some underground paper in Atlanta, Georgia, which was true. The fact that Miranda never thought highly of this person's intelligence or journalistic instinct was something Tasha just forgot to mention.

"Thank you, honey," he said later. "And I will get Sam and Tony to call you," John waived and paid the cabdriver to take her.

"Yeah, right," Tasha muttered to herself.

Chapter six:

A Bumpy Sidetrip Begins

Tasha never thought she would experience the day when she envied all her mere mortal classmates, and how their banal mediocre existence could enable them to return to something close to normalcy within a few weeks. For the goddesses, however, it was an example of how with highs, comes the lows.

Elizabeth and Dawn were overwhelmed with guilt in that they thought they each had the power to prevent such tragedies from occurring. They also felt some guilt in their anger at Miranda for stealing from them in the first place. However, being the good goddesses that they were, they rose to the occasion and provided resilient leadership, making it possible for the campus to continue to function—at least until graduation.

Tasha, too, was the picture of composure, but her strengths came from an excess amount of marijuana, vomiting in the middle of the night, fear of being exposed, her keeping a promise to Miranda, her acting talent, and a new strong desire to keep hold of Elizabeth and Dawn. For reasons, she couldn't explain, Tasha just felt that if the three could stay connected, then everything would be okay. It didn't matter that they were out of the loop, or that they would be horrified by Tasha's secrets; Tasha just knew that birds of a feather, just had to keep flocking together, and these were the only other goddesses that she knew.

On a Thursday evening in May, after her last college final ever, Tasha entered the bathroom to roll yet another joint, and within seconds, she experienced all the classics signs of a heart attack, but still had enough lung power to burst out a chilling scream, which had enough force to propel he body backwards, knocking her into the heater. Gaining composure, she slapped herself on the face to regain some color and then confidently waited until her roommates came dashing in.

"Tasha, are you okay?" Elizabeth said as she bolted in.

"I feel so stupid. I thought I saw a big spider, and it scared the shit out of me."

"Where did you think you saw it?" asked Dawn, who was the type that rescued such creatures as oppose to stomping on them.

"On the floor here, but it was just my comb—don't ask. You had to be here."

"Apparently," Elizabeth said with a teasing smile as the two of them exited.

Tasha waited a few minutes before opening the cabinet again. Gingerly she removed the note, with Miranda's handwriting and the lyrics from Simon and Garfunkles' *Somewhere They Can't Find Me*.

My life seems unreal. My crime, an illusion.

A scene badly written, in which I must play.

But I've got to creep down the alley way.
Fly down the highway.
Before they come to get me, I'll be gone.
Somewhere, they can't find me."

Tasha sat down on the toilet and burnt the note before lighting up. For the first time in weeks she felt okay. Miranda was obviously okay and was handling the situation in her own way and in her own time. Typical Miranda. Tasha just now needed to stay patient and wait for Miranda to let her know what to do next, and God willing, this whole horrid drama would be nearing its epilogue soon. Of course, remaining patient was not one of Tasha's strongsuits, and for the first time in their history, Miranda had the upperhand in the timing.

"Oh God, Miranda, don't use this calamity as a learning tool for me," Tasha begged as she took her first hit. "Don't force a bumpy sidetrip on me."

Chapter seven:

PCU Finale

Tasha sat down on the toilet to smoke the one last joint, on the eve of her graduation, and felt such a combination of mixed emotions that she burst into tears before Elizabeth could even get the little doobie lit.

"It's okay, my dear," the ever-presence earth-mother, Dawn, consoled. "We have all kept up such a brave front for the rest of the campus, that we forgot how we could be honest within this realm."

"Oh don't say that," pleaded Tasha, feeling more guilt than anything.

"Dawn is right. We all need a good cry. I know I was so focused on providing leadership in the unifying process and Dawn was the main facilitator in the healing process."

And I was the schmuck that got us all into this fiasco in the first place, Tasha thought.

"And Tasha was the shining star at the end of the tunnel, the beam that was bringing us hope," Dawn jumped in.

Was she kidding?

"I don't think so." Tasha said softly.

"Tasha stop being so hard on yourself. You, too, Elizabeth. Being goddesses we became so accustomed to controlling our universe that we forgot about all those other forces out there that can and do stir up discourse in our existences. Now, as goddesses, we must remember to work on what we can control and to grant to even a higher power, what we can't control. And what we can't control right now is Miranda's journey, wherever it is. Remember she may not have chosen it, but it may have chosen her and we must let her travel it in her own fashion."

Tasha just sat there tight in a ball.

"And our own journeys, goddesses, well, we will be embarking on them soon," Dawn said taking a hit.

"But I'm afraid of going it alone," Tasha confessed. "I just can't shake that feeling of that undertow stalking me, waiting to grab up and take me down."

"I still feel it, too, Tasha," Elizabeth said. "And I suspect we will feel it for a long time, but, none of us are really going to be alone. Our paths, whether we want them to or not will continue to merge, cross, intertwine, anything but separate. And, I for one am thankful."

"Thank you, Elizabeth. And you too, Dawn. Not many people could handle me for four years."

"Well, you did provide a hell of lot of entertainment," Dawn giggled.

"And we expect you to continue to provide an Elysian sidetrip or two throughout our adult lives," Elizabeth voiced.

"Yeah, but, Tasha, let us get somewhat settled. Maybe around the time of ten-year reunion, I will be ready for another adventure," Dawn teased.

"Well, now you've done it. You challenged me and I'm going to accept it. All I can say, is in nine or ten years from now, be prepared."

Maybe because it was against their nature to end on a sour note, the trio laughed and loved until the next morning when it was time to attire themselves in their gowns and march that last march as Satyr undergrads.

Chapter eight:
Annual Notes

"*To take refuge with an inferior is to betray one's self*." Publius Syrus.

Whoa, Tasha nearly fainted when she read that note on March 10, 1974, backstage at a New York theatre where she was performing.

"Randy," she called over to a stagehand, "where did these flowers come from?"

"Beats me, they were left outside, with a note for you."

"How long ago?"

"Beats me."

Tasha ran outside hoping to spot Miranda or at least her messenger, but was not too surprised to find just an empty alley.

"Well, goddess, it at least appears that you have taken refuge in a safe haven. I'm at least thankful for that," Tasha said wiping away the tears.

A year later, when Tasha was filming a pilot for Sam Cannon—who knew that John Morgan would keep his word—Tasha received another bouquet of flowers. This time the anonymous note read: *In the morning, when the sun rises, sometimes it's hard to believe there was a night."* Joseph Cotton to Ingrid Bergman in *Gaslight*.

"Code. She's content. Leave everything alone," Tasha concluded.

Then the next year, when she was starring in a Tony Winters soap opera—who knew that John Morgan would keep his word twice—she received a copy of her script, with a note stuck inside: *Our patience will achieve more than our force.*

"Damn, goddess, you're good. What are you going to do for an encore?" Well, maybe because Miranda had a whole year to think about it, she always managed to provide something that satisfied Tasha's well-developed subversive streak, and sometimes even amuse her. The best was in 1982 when Tasha received a page from the ten year reunion booklet listing missing classmates, with Miranda's name circled with a happy face.

"Well, time has given you a sense of humor. But obviously, not the desire to come home again," And, Tasha, never known for her patience, once again submitted fully to Miranda's will. But, then what choice did she have?

Chapter nine:

Road to Shangri-La

Granted Tasha was never known for her sense of ethics, but she could keep a promise if she wanted, and she wanted to in the summer of 1982, when she received her 10 year college reunion invitation in the mail.

Tasha immediately placed a call to the chairperson, Elizabeth P. Adams-Miles, esq., complimenting her on the invitation style and to make fun of former classmates. Now somewhere in the conversation, Elizabeth let it slip that she was feeling a bit fatigued.

Well, in normal circumstances, that would not have been a news flash. After all, that would be expected of any mere mortal woman still working full-time as an attorney, caring for her newborn, and chairing the reunion committee. But this wasn't any mere mortal woman. This was, after all, Elizabeth, fellow goddess in college, and now the prototype of the modern woman, the personification of the Protestant work ethic, the envy of all her upper scale neighbors. So when she admitted to feeling fatigued, well, it was indeed, a news flash.

Most friends of the above-mentioned woman would have quickly offered condolences and even volunteered to perform some of the more tedious tasks for the upcoming reunion. But this was Tasha. And Tasha never had much use for those pedestrian suggestions. Her responses to problems and situations were always somewhat more Sybaritic. Plus she owed Elizabeth a journey or a sidetrip at least.

"Oh Christ, Tasha, you are still such a hedonist. I cannot just drop everything and take off for a health spa for three days." Elizabeth lectured in a motherly way.

"Why not? You've been functioning like one of those worker ants in that fable. It's time to enjoy the fruits of your labor."

"I know I'm going to regret asking this, but what the hell are you getting at?"

"You've been going on full-throttle for this past year. I mean, you were back after one week of Heather's birth."

"I was just picking up some papers to review."

"And it was three days before you left. Now, let's face it. You're not going to get any rest in your current environment."

"And I would get some in yours?"

"Hell, no. That's why we have to leave. Come on, one weekend. Sleep in; get a facial, a massage. Eat healthy. This trip will rejuvenate your spirits, and enhance your energy level, thus enabling you to pull off the mother of all class reunions. You will set the standard for all Parnassus Canyon University class reunions."

When Elizabeth did not jump back immediately with a rebuttal, Tasha knew she was rounding second, going for third, and to make this a homerun, she pulled out the hidden ace card.

"We'll kidnap Dawn and take her with us."

"Now you've blown it, Tasha," Elizabeth laughed. "I know for a fact Dawn can't make it. Two toddlers and a new mortgage. She's been saving what she can for this reunion."

Tasha was almost in a state of panic, thinking she should have settled at this point for a triple, but, but in a calm voice, she used an old tactic. "Well, if she agrees, will you?"

"Yes. But she has to call me herself. And no lies, or tricks to convince her."

"Moi?"

"I'm your ex-roommate, remember. God, it's a miracle, you can still talk me into these things."

"Au contraire. It's a blessing." Tasha then hung up and called Dawn Callie Wolfe, PhD, and as predicted, Dawn did relate her financial concerns; but, if anyone could make a weekend at a health spa sound like a constitutional right, it was Tasha, and by the end of that evening, Tasha had been given the go ahead to make reservations at a local, reasonably priced spa for the three of them.

"Damn. You are good, "Tasha's husband, Jacob, marveled.

"Damn. I'm a goddess," she reminded him, as she began checking out local spas.

"This unique east-west valley with mystical powers was captured in 1937 when Frank Capra used the mountain vistas as the mythical Shangri-La in his film, *The Lost Horizon*," she read aloud with excitement from the brochure.

Tasha then sent off a note to her friends. Clotho, Lachesis, and Atropos (the sister fates for those of you who cannot remember Freshman Humanities) have spoken. We're going to Shangri-La. We're going to Ojai.

Thus a tradition was born. For the next nine years in September, the three would leave jobs, spouses, and children, not necessarily in that order, and convene at the Shangri-La Spa in Ojai, a small quaint town, northeast of Los Angeles, for a weekend of good health, good friends, and good gossip.

Well, you certainly kept your promise back then," Elizabeth said in the jacuzzi. But next year, is our 20th reunion. What the hell are you going to do for us then?"

"Well, I have a year to think about," Tasha wiggled her eyebrows.

"Personally, I just love coming here. I vote for no change," offered Dawn. "As far as I am concerned, this tradition could carry on for an eternity on the same level of tranquility."

"Watch out, Dawn" Tasha interjected. "I have learned that the ever whimsical Hermes, can get bored by a long sense of complacency, and he just might toss us a curve that would set in motion one hell of a journey to Elysium and back."

"Well, if he does. Who better to have in the driver seat, than you?" Elizabeth laughed.

"Just hope you two still think that way when it's over," said Tasha leaning back, hiding the fact that she felt a sense of impending chaos.

Chapter ten:

Goddesses on the Wall

Tasha was usually not one who found joy in banality but when Miranda's annual communiqués became tedious and somewhat repetitious, she postulated that it signified a sense of peace in Miranda's realm wherever that was. In fact, in March of 1991, Tasha forgot about all about the annual event, until the UPS man woke her up bright and early, only to deliver a poster size print of the *Realm of the Goddesses* picture taken their first night in the dorm. Then the following year, the UPS man delivered a framed copy of the beautiful Reuben's *Judgment of Paris,* depicting Paris having to choose between Hera, Athena, and Aprhrodite.

"All because that Eros threw in that little apple," laughed Tasha. "Well, Miranda, if you thought you created a little discord for us, well, goddess, you were right."

Tasha then knew that for the past few years, Miranda had been easy on her, in order for her to store up her energy, as the nature of the game was soon going to change. Miranda, no doubt, was going to steer her in a new direction and where she landed, would be anyone's guess. Strange, Tasha found herself almost giddy with excitement. "Fade-in" she laughed as she lit up a joint while admiring her two new favorite wall hangings.

Chapter eleven:

Road to Shangri-La: The Sequel

"Fade-in," Jacob instructed his hand-picked, Director Guild Association trainee, who also happened to be his nine- year-old son, Eli, on that Friday morning of September 4th 1992, Eli sturdily held the camera, his mother, Tasha, opened the front door and sashayed down the cobblestone walk that led to the street. Her daughter, Caprice, 11, provided the narration:

"And here is the lovely and award-winning actress, Tasha Felding, preparing for her annual jaunt to the Shangri-La Spa in Ojai, where she will be joined by Aunt Elizabeth and Aunt Dawn in honor of their impending 20 year college reunion."

Eli's twin sister, Shilo, took over the voice-over. "Never one to make a subtle entrance, Tasha Felding will be arriving in." Then Tasha and her two daughters quickly stood in front of the rented 1988 red convertible corvette.

"There they are, those fabulous Felding females," Jacob bragged. And on cue, the three waved and blew kisses toward the camera, before launching into a high-kick dance routine "Fade-out. That's a wrap," Jacob announced.

As offspring of an actress and a TV director, the three children were at home around movie lingo as military children were around a 24-hour time table.

"Now everyone get ready for school," the director barked.

Tasha who had packed lunches, ironed uniforms, etc. the night before, stood by her beloved car as the kids got themselves ready and off to school that Friday morning. She was still by the car when Jacob came running out the door with keys in mouth while zipping up his brief case. Throwing his stuff into the BMW, he quickly ran over to kiss Tasha and wish her a good time.

"I always have fun looking for my inner child," she taunted.

Jacob stopped in his tracks and slowly returned to her. "It's not the discovery of your inner child that scares me. It's the inner adolescent. Or even worse, the inner college coed."

"Now darling no need to worry. You know that little coed is like a homing pigeon who always returns home," she said in hopes of reassuring him.

"But not without some interesting detours at times," Jacob reminded her.

She looked at him. Every once in a while, he felt threatened and this was one of those times. Together on and off for 22 years and married 10, they shared a history that was a rich and tumultuous as the late 1960's, but neither would change a moment of it. It was no secret to anyone who knew them that it was the emergence of AIDS that had kept them pretty monogamous since the mid 1980's. Dawn phrased it best, when she described them as each other's match.

Tasha reached out and hugged her husband. "Don't worry, dear. Ojai is for my sense of peace, not adventure. I have never even had a close call there."

Jacob stood back a bit and studied the car. "With this fine machine under your fine ass, this may be the ultimate test."

"You don't think I'll pass?"

"Honey, you were never a good student. But no matter what happens."

"What?" Tasha asked.

"Bring this car back in one piece. You're expensive enough to keep as it is without upping our insurance premium," Jacob lectured.

"I could take you for a test drive," she teased.

"No, but..." he said with a wicked look in his eyes that accelerated Tasha's pulse.

Jacob grabbed on to her waist and mounted her atop the hood. Then he dropped to his knees and lifted her silk broomstick pleated skirt up to her hips. "Yes," he howled. "No underwear. Babe, you never let me down." And right then and there he placed his head under the skirt and proceeded to give her one fond farewell that would hopefully cancel out any temptation she might encounter that weekend.

She was still sitting on the car, when he pulled out of the driveway licking his lips.

"Fade-out," she purred.

A couple of hours later, with Meatloaf's *Bat Out of Hell* blaring from her tape player, she was off and running. By the time Meatloaf was seducing his date in *Paradise by the Dashboard Light,* she was exiting the 405 and entering 101, aka the Ventura Freeway, which obviously meant it was time for America's Greatest Hits and a listen to *Ventura Highway*. Entering highway 33, she opted for some Uriah Heap, especially *Easy Livin'*. It was while rewinding this song that Tasha knocked over her iced tea and recalling what Jacob had said about taking care of the car, she pulled over to wipe it clean.

She was about to reenter the road when she noticed that she was the only car around, which was quite uncommon for this time and place. Figuring that there had to be some higher purpose for this, she leaned back and placed her feet up on the steering wheel so she could enjoy the serenity of it all. Suddenly feeling a little wicked, she turned up the volume a bit, stretched her arms up and then brought them down to her knees, and slowly slid them up to her inner thighs. Giggling a little, she almost wished that Jacob hadn't presented her with such a fine bon voyage gift.

"Are you okay, Miss?"

Tasha must have broken some Guinness World Book record with her jump before turning to the inquiring stranger. "Yes, I'm fine," she stammered before realizing that he too, was fine. Quite fine as a matter of fact. She quickly surmised that he must have been in his early thirties, about 5'8", medium built, but no stranger to nautilus, brown hair, long in the back, shiny blue eyes, and a mustache which somewhat camouflaged what must had been a severe case of acne. He was attired in a white t-shirt, at least one size too small under a black leather jacket, and a pair of jeans which he probably put on with a crow bar. In his arm was a helmet. Tasha discreetly glanced behind and was not surprised to see a Harley-Davidson.

"Better be careful, lady. It's hard to stay anywhere near the speed limit with Uriah Heep pumping the adrenaline." She made a move to change the tape. "Now, wait, I didn't say be to a fanatic. I said just be careful," he advised, winking at her. She thought about the conversation she just had with her husband and wondered if this was going to be the test. But before she could worry even more, the son of Bronson sauntered back to his bike and mounted it. She was about to pull out when he pulled up beside her.

"Bachman Turner Overdrive would sound good, too."

She laughed and pulled out her BTO tape from the glove compartment. "I think you and I are on the same wavelength," she said in all innocence.

"I know we are," the stranger smiled. And Tasha knew he was not referring to their similar taste in classic rock. Winking again, he put on his helmet and headed off into the horizon.

Tasha watched his departure with a mixture of relief and disappointment.

"Fade-out," she sighed.

Chapter twelve:

Let The Games Begin

Concurrently in Ojai, a newly-leased white Mercedes SL driven by Elizabeth with Dawn as co-pilot, pulled into the Shangri-La Spa's parking lot. After checking in, the two decided to take advantage of the calm before the storm and walk around the peaceful bohemian little town.

As they headed back to the spa, they saw a red corvette piloted by some wild-hair desperado heading into town.

"I wonder if she picked up Buz and Tod along the way," Elizabeth laughed.

"God, I would never tell Jacob this, but she looks at home in that thing," said Dawn enviously.

"Please don't tell her that, either. We do have to live with her this weekend," pleaded Elizabeth.

As Tasha maneuvered her large toy into the parking lot, the other two jumped on top of the hood and presented their best car show modeling poses to the appreciative audience—mostly pedestrians who were forced to wait as the car found itself a resting place.

"Okay, okay, girls," Tasha announced, "good show. You were beautiful. You can pick up your checks at the office. Come prepared to give the boss a blow job."

"Is that clause in the standard car show modeling contract?" inquired the attorney.

"It was always in mine."

"Tasha, good to see you," Dawn said as she hugged her. "Michael and the kids say hi."

"And everyone in Marin sends their love," added Elizabeth as she joined the hugging session.   Elizabeth then walked around the car. "So a little drag racing later?"

"We can do whatever we want with it, as long as it looks normal when I return home. I got a major lecture regarding insurance premiums. Jacob is not too thrilled by this."

"What!" Elizabeth mockingly exclaimed, "You mean he's not too thrilled that you're driving this 'Yes I still have a sex drive' car in this horny artistic community?"

"Yeah, can you imagine that?"

"Let's see, Tasha's driving a red corvette, Elizabeth's lusting after some easy rider. Boy, am I a bit delayed for mid-life crisis here or what?" joked Dawn.

"Elizabeth is lusting after easy rider? What? What gives here?" Tasha obviously had not heard enough.

"Oh nothing, Dawn is just joking around," Elizabeth said in an attempt to bring closure to the subject.

"Exuse moi, my beloved attorney, this one here is not known for joking around, but her keen observation skills—me thinks there's a good scandal here."

"You're going to be so disappointed," offered Elizabeth.

"Probably not," offered Dawn.

"Then give, come on, give."

"It's really no big deal," Elizabeth insisted.

"Hey, when an attorney describes something as no big deal, it's a big deal. Dawn, spill it."

"Christ," Elizabeth griped.

"All I know is that I walked into a bookstore while Elizabeth waited outside, and all of a sudden, I heard squealing breaks."

"A car ran a red light and almost hit a motorcyclist," Elizabeth interrupted.

"Oh my god," Tasha said expecting the worse.

"Don't worry, everything turned out okay," Dawn reassured her. "The driver was embarrassed of course, but the cyclist just smiled and waved to the driver, as if saying, hey no harm done. We've all been there."

"Wow, what a saint," Tasha said.

"Well, if he is, this one is about to convert. You've should have seen her. I was expecting her to chase after him," Dawn teased.

"Only if he wants custody of his kids. I've managed to avoid personal injury suits thus far, and I'm not going to start now. Not even for that motorcyclist."

"That motorcyclist?" stated Dawn.

"Yes, that motorcyclist," responded Elizabeth.

"Significant description."

"And what would be so insignificant," asked the confused lawyer.

"THE motorcyclist."

"Semantics. I don't really see a difference."

"Well, *the* is general. *That* is specific," explained Dawn.

"There was only one motorcyclist, ergo, he was *that* specific man on a cycle," counter argued the lawyer.

"And I'm sure you could pick him out in a line up?"

"Well, first, has he been charged with anything?"

"Just getting to you."

"Pardon?"

"Getting to you."

"Now, Dawn, I believe you would be hard-pressed to convince any jury of that"

"Ah, but I am privy to some other evidence."

"Which you have an obligation to share."

"So I will. I exited the bookstore just as everything was happening."

"So you witnessed a near-accident?"

"I witnessed you. You were transfixed."

"I was not."

"Were too."

"Dawn, I thought I was witnessing a fatal collision. I was paying attention in case I was subpoenaed."

"What kind of car ran the red light?" Dawn crossed her arms.

It was obvious to Tasha that Elizabeth had no clue.

"Describe the person driving the car?" Dawn remained still with her arms crossed.

"Okay. I guess I was focusing on THAT motorcyclist, but I thought he was dead meat. I don't apologize for it."

Dawn smiled at her friend. "You were transfixed.

Tasha viewed their verbal volley, wondering if this particular easy rider could also be her easy rider from a few hours ago. That would be one hell of a coincidence.

"Tasha, you're an expert at checking out men. Would you tell Dawn that I was not..."

"Sorry, Goddess, Dawn won this volley. But then it's not too surprising. You always did have a thing for the *Wild One* and the *Wild Angels*."

"Tasha, don't you need to get checked in or something?" Elizabeth said with some resignation.

"Sure. Come on. And Dawn, don't worry. If' it's a mid-life crisis you're craving. I'll get you on your way."

"Please, Tasha," Dawn moaned, "I'm still recovering from college days."

"But, Tasha, you can relax. Your picture is still on the celebrity wall," Elizabeth reassured her.

"Good," Tasha gave her Emmy winning smile.

"And Wendy told us that many guests recognize you, especially from your soap days," Dawn continued with the therapeutic touch as they entered the spa.

"I kept telling those bastards not to kill off my character. Sure it won the sweeps period and me the Emmy. But they have suffered ever since."

"Hello, Mrs. Felding, so nice to see you again," the ever-perky Wendy greeted them. "Did you complete that movie about the priest killing that family?"

"Oh yeah. From today's headlines. It will be on during the November sweeps. How about you? How's the career going?"

"Better. Thanks to you and your husband. I worked twice with him last year and now have a SAG card. He's great."

"I thought the runt's nickname was Napoleon."

"Oh, he's a tough taskmaster, no doubt about it. But he gets the best performance out of everybody. Would love to work with him again. Is he busy with anything?"

Tasha paused. She had promised Jacob that she would quit sending spa employees to his casting agents. But what the hell, Wendy had been a sweetheart to them for the past couple of years, and besides, she had worked with him already, so she was, in a sense, not sending a spa employee, but a bona-fide SAG card carrying actress.

"He's working on a few things with Sam Cannon, both in L.A. and in Vancouver. Give Colleen, his casting director a call and tell her that Maureen, Jacob's assistant is sending you. Plus, I'll call Colleen myself."

As Wendy instructed someone to take Tasha's bags to their room, Tasha could feel the icy stares of her friends upon her.

"Okay, okay. I know I promised Jacob I would no longer send him stray cats, but this is Wendy."

"You're just a soft touch," laughed Elizabeth.

"And you never take a case pro bono?" Dawn reminded her.

"Sure, but then I turn around and overcharge my paying clients."

"Which means, you can spring for the margaritas and salsa?" Tasha announced. "I hereby officially declare these games open." And the three of them headed across the street to the Mexican restaurant for what they always

referred to as the opening ceremony:
margaritas, chips, and salsa.

Chapter thirteen:

The Games

Most health and fitness experts would not advise anyone to take a step aerobic class following an afternoon of margaritas and salsa, but Ojai tended to make its own rules and when in Ojai.

Tasha and Dawn, barely making it on time, giggled and tripped as they entered the exercise room just as the young nubile instructor, Dani, was introducing herself.

"With an i?" asked Tasha.

"Why, yes," answered Dani in a saccharine voice, which only caused Tasha to burst out laughing, which in turn, caused Dani to inform the two that there were less challenging classes available, and that the spa was substance-free.

Tasha, then, informed Dani that she had danced for 72 hours straight at Woodstock, with every kind of substance in her system. It looked as if it was going to get even uglier, when Elizabeth waltzed in and gracefully requested that the class get started.

With their exercise class behind them, the three went to dinner and somewhat enjoyed the low-fat, low-calorie, high-protein cuisine for which the spa was famous. Afterwards, they munched on yogurt-covered pretzels and diet sodas that they had smuggled in and read the tacky tabloids, compliments of Tasha.

Saturday morning came too early, but none the less, the three rose and took part in the six mile hike into the Topa Topa Mountains. The hike was followed by a stretch class, which was followed by a low-fat, low-calorie, high-protein breakfast. That afternoon was dedicated to shopping in town, lunch out, facials and another step aerobic class.

For mere mortals that would have been an exhausting day, completed with an early lights out. But thanks to Tasha's contagious exuberance, the three still possessed enough energy for their annual trek to *The Bacchanal*, the best rock and roll bar in the Ventura triangle.

When they reached *The Bacchanal*, Tasha gingerly parked the corvette between two vans, hoping the vans would conceal the car from would-be thieves and that van owners were by nature responsible family people, therefore, they would not dent the car. Elizabeth and Dawn did not follow the logic at all.

Stepping inside, Tasha, as usual decided she needed one last look in the mirror before making her entrance. "I'm sorry. This will only take a minute. Either one of you coming?"

"No, we're not required to look ravishing carrying your train," Elizabeth said with a hint of sarcasm.

"Amusing. But remember, your thrill of a lifetime could be in that bar as we speak."

"Which is why we would like to enter it sometime this century," snapped Dawn.

"Okay, okay, I'm going."

As usual, Tasha took more than a minute. And as usual, Elizabeth decided she would use the restroom one last time, so she wouldn't have to later. And as usual, Dawn got bored with waiting and went in and claimed a table by herself.

As Tasha and Elisabeth made their way to the table, Tasha stopped cold in her tracks, forcing Elizabeth to bump into her.

"Cattle crossing or something?" Elizabeth growled.

"Oh, ah, nothing. I just thought a waiter was coming through. Sorry," Tasha stammered.

It was not a waiter at all that had caused Tasha to fumble, but Dawn. Earlier that day, Tasha felt a jolt of euphoric rush thanks to the tight jeans of some guy on a Harley. Later in the day, Elizabeth, in Dawn's words, became transfixed on some guy on a motorcycle. Now Dawn, too, appeared to be mesmerized by a pair of tight jeans. Unfortunately, the jeans and the man who wore them made their exit before Tasha could get a better view of him.

"Miranda?" Tasha whispered to herself.

"What did you say?" asked Elizabeth. "Did you say what I thought you said?"

"Yeah, see that woman over there; don't you think she's looks like Miranda?"

"Well, if you squint just right," Elizabeth answered sarcastically.

"A simple no would have sufficed," Tasha reminded her.

Of course, Elizabeth didn't think that woman looked like Miranda. She didn't. Not even close. But it just made more sense than trying to explain the presence of some apple being tossed at them by some long lost roommate. But, of course, none of this interfered with the three of them staying out late and having a great time.

As it does every year, Sunday morning came too soon. But as they do every year, the trio rose to the occasion and took another six mile hike, followed by a stretch class and breakfast. That afternoon featured pedicures and a yoga class.

Resting in their room before dinner, Tasha and Elizabeth enjoyed the tabloids again while Dawn picked up the ice.

"Here we are," she said entering the room, "Cold ice for Tasha's pulled hamstring. By the way, Dani with an i says she is sorry you're hurt and recommends some of the less challenging classes in the future."

"Great, now I'm being pitied by a bimbette."

"We must all make sacrifices for the greater good," said Elizabeth as she chilled the bottle of Dom Perion that she brought.

"Now let me get this straight. We agreed to take turns, being the so-called injured party, but each year, I am the one in need of the ice. Why?" asked Tasha.

"Because, you're an actress, and you can't resist a part." answered Elizabeth. "But you would think that after ten years, they would have noticed the pattern. Every Sunday, we need ice. Oh well."

"Dinner time, Elizabeth. Miss Felding, showtime," Dawn announced. And Tasha walked out with her best *my hamstring is killing me* limp.

Upon entering their room after dinner, Elizabeth popped the cork, and Dawn berated Tasha for continuously switching her so-called hurt leg just to confuse Dani.

"Oh, come on, you enjoyed witnessing her feeble mind in action trying to figure it out," Tasha said.

"Sisterhood at its best," Dawn lamented. "Champagne ready?"

"Here it is. Okay, Goddesses, a toast. To another wonderful weekend in Ojai." Elizabeth said.

"God, I love it here. I love drinking champagne here," giggled Tasha. "Makes me feel as if I'm breaking the dorm's rule."

"We are breaking the dorm's rule," Elizabeth reminded her.

"Well I wouldn't want to let my fellow classmates down. God, I can't believe we've been out of college for almost twenty years. Well here's to our reunion and our classmates showing up heavier and poorer."

"Knock if off, Tasha," Dawn scolded. "We have all done well and I think we can wish some good fortune on our friends. Right, Elizabeth?"

"I agree." Elizabeth paused for a moment before seriously speaking again. "You know, we have all accomplished quite a bit, not only in college, but since graduation."

"Oh shit, Dawn, I know this tone. She's gone off and won another award. What is it this time? Mrs. America?"

"Oh it can't be that, Tasha. That's one you have to actually apply for. Elizabeth specializes in those exclusive trophies chosen by a committee. So what specific Nobel were you granted?"

"That's enough. Now listen, I'm very excited about this award. Probably more excited than..."

"All your other awards?" Tasha asked sarcastically.

"Well, yes. But this is one in which I want to share with you. I want you to be part of it."

"First and second runner ups. In the event that you cannot complete..." Tasha started.

"Knock it off, Tasha," Dawn scowled. "Okay Elizabeth, break it to us gently. What award are you receiving?"

Elizabeth stood in the center of the room and proudly announced, "The Parnassus Canyon University, Walter Tudor's Outstanding Alumnus Award."

The other two threw up their pillows and applauded and whistled.

"So is there a cash prize or do you get your picture in the yearbook again?" asked Tasha.

"Well, if either one of you had served on the reunion committee or participated in the Alumni Association..."

"In which you are past president," jumped in Dawn.

"Then you would know that this award is not given annually, and the recipient is awarded with a hall or wing, or something named after her."

"Do you know what it is yet?" Tasha asked.

"No. And I won't know until they announce it at our reunion cocktail party. But for me, the big thrill is that this year, the committee asked me back for the entire Homecoming/Reunion week, you know to visit, and inspire current students."

"So are you going to do it?" asked Dawn.

"Of course. The firm can do without me for a week. And guess where I'm going to stay?"

"Dean Becvar's bed?" Tasha smirked.

"No, you common whore, our old room."

"Tudor, 407?" screeched Tasha. "Elizabeth, this is a reward, not a punishment!"

"I thought Tudor Hall was no longer a dorm, that it was being converted into an administrative building," said Dawn.

"It is. But it's only half-done. The first floor is the switchboard and a copying center. The second floor now houses some of the Deans' offices. But the third, fourth and fifth floors haven't been touched. The rooms are still intact."

"Aren't you afraid of being there alone?" Dawn asked.

"For openers, the switchboards and copying center are open 24 hours. Second of all, and this took me by surprised, President Riley thought it would make a great human interest story, and generate a great deal of publicity if you two joined me. Now, you both were planning to be there by Friday of that week. Do you suppose you could show up Monday, and have the families meet you Friday?"

"Wait. You're suggesting that I sleep in Tudor 407 again," exclaimed Tasha.

"You hardly slept there when it was your official address," teased Dawn.

"Yeah, Tasha," Elizabeth winked at Dawn, "for old times sake, I suppose I could arrange for you to sleep with a different football player or lead actor each night."

"Laugh all you want, you Philistines," Tasha said throwing pillows at her friends. "It was the time. And you have to admit, I was the best soldier in the sexual revolution."

"Hell, you were a four star general," Elizabeth saluted.

"And do I have some war stories."

"But let us not forget, that it was our own Elizabeth P. Adams who led the crusade for birth control pills to be distributed at health services. Or who openly supported legalized abortions," Dawn reminded them.

"And the Equal Rights Amendment. And let's not forget the support of the Wounded Knee seizure and the denouncement of the Vietnam War," Tasha chimed in.

"You took some strong stands back then. I remember a few trustees were not happy when you were elected student president for our senior year," Dawn said.

"And I have the battle scars to prove it but all those battles and confrontations with conservative trustees, uptight parents, and even fellow students, prepared me for the courtroom. I got a lot out of that university."

"So did I," reflected Dawn.

"So. Don't you think we owe to our younger sisters, and even brothers, to be there, and to let them know that the idealism and dreams they have today that can create a strong foundation for their futures. In fact, I want all those young bucks to know that we are just not legends, but are also in our prime."

Tasha found herself in a quandary. Paranoia had prevented her from ever participating in any kind of PCU related publicity and paranoia was going to prevail again. But she hadn't a clue as how to get out of it without insulting Elizabeth or, ironically, bringing attention to herself.

"Elizabeth, you know I love you and I would do anything for you, but I just can't do this right now," Dawn said solemnly.

"Thank you fates," Tasha said very softly.

"Dawn what do you mean you can't?" asked Elizabeth, genuinely surprised.

"First, I don't consider myself a legend, and I am anything but in my prime."

"What are you talking about? You have taken your education back to your roots. Your career counseling programs. Your intervention programs. Your teen pregnancy prevention program."

"My working twice the hours, with half the results. My grant proposals not getting submitted in time."

"That's not your fault, Dawn," Elizabeth interjected.

"My new programs not succeeding because they are not being implemented as planned."

"Again, not your fault," Elizabeth demanded. "I keep telling you, you need to allow yourself to be considered for an administrative job. You're a natural," Elizabeth said.

"No, I'm not. At one point, I think I was a good therapist for the agency. But I don't know, I think, well, hell, I don't want to get into it."

"Listen, Dawn, you sound a little burned out. I know this sounds selfish, but why don't you take the week off and give yourself some space to reevaluate," Elizabeth pleaded.

"I'm in the process of reevaluating now, but I just can't desert the troops. We are so understaffed now that to take a week off would be quite unfair. I'll just see you that Friday," Dawn said with a hint of sadness in her voice.

"I didn't realize you were feeling so blue," Elizabeth said, handing Dawn another glass of champagne.

"I didn't mean to ruin our weekend. Don't worry, I'll be okay. Hell, it seems I'm having a mid-life crisis after all, except I'm too boring to do something like rent a corvette. I have to experience job burn out," Dawn said fighting back the tears, and giggling at her weak joke.

"Dawn, it's okay. You have a tough job. You wear a lot of hats." Tasha said with her arms around her.

"Don't you see? I can't do the week with you two. I would feel like a real loser. I know you can't relate," Dawn said, still battling with the tears.

"Actually Dawn, I can," said Tasha. "You know that stupid TV movie that Wendy mentioned. Well, hell, that's been my one and only real part in about two years."

"But, I've seen you on TV," Dawn said through the tears.

"On all of Sam Cannon's action shows right? Directed by my husband, right? With my one token scene. God bless Sam. Without him, I don't know. He has kept both me and Jacob employed over the years."

"Especially Jacob, I hardly watch TV, but when I do, there's that credit which says directed by Jacob Felding. At least he's busy, and you can be there for the kids?" Dawn said.

"Kids are getting older, not to mention, sick of me. And part of our agreement, was that Jacob would sell out and make the money in TV for awhile and then I was to pick up the slack, so he could cut back, and return to his roots, dangerous, rebellious experimental theatre."

"But the Kaleidoscope Company is still going. And he's on the Board," Elizabeth pointed out.

"Which means he donates some of his TV money to the cause. He really would like to direct again here and there. Maybe even write his own play." Tasha took another sip of Champagne and then braced herself. "Listen, Elizabeth, maybe it's best that you hog the spotlight on this one. I mean, you are the outstanding alumnus."

Elizabeth sat down and refilled her own glass. Tasha could tell that she was not giving up. At least, not yet.

"I forgot to mention, they hired a highly-regarded documentary filmmaker to produce a recruiting film. And he wants to include footage of the three of us back on campus."

"Elizabeth, I just can't. I would be a fraud," Dawn said very firmly.

"You understand, don't you?" Tasha asked carefully and full of guilt.

"I guess," Elizabeth pouted.

There was an awkward pregnant pause, broken only when Dawn picked up their senior yearbook.

"Oh wow, haven't looked at that in a while," Tasha said trying to change both subject and atmosphere. "Look, George Weybourne."

"One of your many conquests," teased Dawn. "Didn't the two of you go down to Mexico over spring break our junior year?"

"Yes, they did," Elizabeth jumped in, "however, Tasha told her Dad that she was spending the week with my family in Beverly Hills. My father still has hearing loss from that conversation he had with your father. And then my father turned and yelled at me, thinking I was part of the conspiracy."

"You were," Tasha reminded her.

"I know. But I wasn't going to tell him that. Thank God, you were a well-known liar back then."

"Apparently I was," Tasha said, remembering Miranda's words that awful night.

"So what other mementos did you bring, Dawn?" asked Elizabeth.

"Scrapbooks. Lord, I haven't looked at them in ages." Dawn picked one up and as she opened it, note paper, plus an old carton of Marlboro cigarettes fell out, which caused Tasha to gasp.

"I know the dates are rough to take, Tasha, you okay?" Dawn asked.

"Yes, champagne went down a wrong pipe or something," she said as she nonchalantly picked up the cigarette box.

"What's all that, Dawn?" Elizabeth asked.

"Oh my God. This is weird. It's some of Miranda's notes, for her articles regarding the Rape Awareness Seminar. What's so intriguing, Tasha?"

"This old cigarette box. Inside there's a name and phone number. Either one of you know a Jack Schwartz?"

"I do," volunteered Elizabeth. "At least, I think I do. Wasn't he a detective with the Topanga Sheriff Department? Not one of those jerks who got in trouble, but one of those who use to work with ASB regarding security issues."

"I recall that name now," Dawn said. "Miranda mentioned something about him speaking at one of the Rape Awareness meetings. I don't think he ever did though."

"Well, as you recalled, not much happened with that project at the end," Elizabeth reflected.

Tasha thought about why that name sounded so familiar. And then it hit her. John Morgan had mentioned that last name along with a few others as officers he wanted far away from the case as possible.

"I wonder why all this stuff is in here? Shit," Dawn growled, "I guess it's been here all along," Dawn mentioned.

I know it is strange that Miranda would put it there. Do you think she thought it was her scrapbook or something?" wondered Elizabeth.

"Or maybe since we both were on the committee," Dawn proposed "she handed it to me, and I placed it in here. Shit, I don't know."

A sense of dreaded silence took over the room for a few moments."

"You know to this day, I just don't get it," Elizabeth admitted. "I have no idea of what made her snap."

"Me either," confessed Dawn.

"What do you mean, 'snap'?" asked Tasha in total disbelief. "You two don't actually think she did it. I mean, not for one minute." Their silence and still bodies answered that question.

"Oh, come on! We stood together in a united front of support for Miranda."

"We were good roommates. We were willing to believe innocent until proven guilty," Elizabeth said.

"And when in the fuck was she proven guilty?"

"Maybe because she failed to show up for the trial," Elizabeth said rather firmly.

"Maybe because she was scared. You said yourself; she got a lot of sheriffs in trouble."

Elizabeth stood in an authoritative pose. "Listen, Tasha, I know. I too wanted to believe she was innocent. Which is why I began to look into the case some years ago."

"You did? I didn't know that?" Tasha said.

"I don't admit to it much. Tasha, I looked at evidence. I spoke with people. Because of my being a lawyer, and my family being good friends with the Morgans, I was able to investigate leads others couldn't. And you know what?" Elizabeth said in a tearful voice.

"What?" Tasha asked not really wanting to hear the answer.

"All roads lead to Rome. Everything leads to her doing it. Trust me. I was devastated. And so I called Dawn."

"What?" Tasha shrieked. Somehow she felt victim of a conspiracy.

"And I asked for her professional opinion, as a psychologist, if she felt there were..."

"And I hope to hell, you told her no," Tasha stated.

"Tasha," Dawn said quietly, placating, "I was closer to Miranda than either you two, or in fact, anyone else. One, because we were both scholarship students, and two, because of the Rape Awareness Project. Tasha, the whole purpose for the project was to educate and create awareness. Well, as our senior year progressed, Miranda, became more and more of a vigilante. She demanded that we named names, that we helped victims in the lawsuits against the school." Dawn shook her head. "And when she was kicked off the committee, she accused us of conspiring with the rapists and that we were forcing her to take matters into her own hands. She vowed to put an end to the rapes."

"She was kicked off." Another surprise for Tasha.

"She was devastated so we all agreed to not advertise that, but she was blocking our progress." Tears welled in Dawn's eyes. "Maybe, that's why this is so hard for me. Maybe we pushed her to murder."

Tasha felt bad. Knowing how sensitive Dawn was, it was logical she would take some of the responsibility. But Tasha was also angry.

"First, Dawn. You cannot blame yourself at all. And second of all, hello, remember me, the third remaining roommate? Why wasn't I included in these conversations?"

Elizabeth and Dawn just stared at her as if the answer was obvious.

"Sorry, Tasha, there was never any intention to exclude you. I guess it just never occurred to me to ask you anything," Dawn said apologetically.

"Let's face it; it's not a pleasant subject. And quite frankly, Tasha, what could you have added?" Elizabeth challenged her.

"Excuse me?"

"You know what I mean. I can bring a legal prospective and Dawn can bring a psychological prospective but you..."

"I'm just an actress?"

"An award-winning actress. But cruel realities are not your forte," Elizabeth said in an unintentional condescending manner.

"Well, fuck, what do you keep me around for?"

And once again the two of them looked at her as if the answer was obvious.

"For the ride," Elizabeth said.

"I mean, who else can create the little sidetrips from everyday boring realty like you," asked Dawn.

Tasha clutched the Marlboro box and leaned over with her arms crossed. "Well, goddesses, you better hold on tight. We're about to embark."

Chapter fourteen:

Checking Out

"Well, Ojai has survived you three once again," said Peter, the cute waiter at Gatekeeper, as he opened the traditional end of the retreat bottle of wine. "I assume you did your usual damage."

"Tasha wouldn't know. She still keeps her eyes shut as she signs her name," Elizabeth said.

"I can't believe you always do that," Dawn said.

"Oh, trust me, I find out soon enough when Jacob gets the bill."

"Dawn," Elizabeth said, pointing to Tasha. I rest my case."

"Not this, 'Tasha can't face reality' shit again," Tasha griped.

"Just making an observation, my dear."

The three began to debate that whole issue once again, when some clumsy oaf stumbled by and knocked over the bottle of wine that was just opened.

"God damn. Excuse me. Here let me clean up," the oaf said, grabbing a napkin, plus a chair to sit in.

"Shit," Tasha said as she looked over at her personal Harley Davidson road buddy. She glanced at Elizabeth and Dawn and quickly surmised that he was also their mystery man. Tasha fought back a naughty giggle as she realized that for the first time in their history, they were all lusting over the same guy. The only difference was that she would actually admit to lusting after him; the other two would try to conjure some logical explanation as to why their hearts were beating double time, their hands were slightly shaking, and their consciousness were anywhere but on planet earth.

"There, that's better," the man said as he finished wiping the table, not that anyone of them noticed. "And don't worry, I'll order another bottle."

"And yourself a glass," Tasha flirted.

"Well aren't you nice?" he said winking at her, indicating that he recognized her also. "So what is this triumvirate raising their glasses to?" he asked.

"Our upcoming college reunion," Elizabeth jumped in, resembling a giddy seventh grader.

"Ten years already?" he asked with some sense of sincerity.

"Well, aren't you nice," Tasha responded in her saucy, she knew bullshit when she heard it manner.

"We hate to admit it, but it will be our 20th," Elizabeth volunteered, still a bit giggly.

"Parnassus Canyon University?" he asked.

"Exactly, why did you guess that?"

"I'm Roger. I'm a starving filmmaker who has been paying the rent these few months thanks to your alma mater," he said extending his hand.

"So you're." Elizabeth started.

"The pesty camera nerd who will to follow you around all week on campus." He then looked at Tasha and then Dawn. "So are you two fellow goddesses going to be there for the worship, also?"

"Definitely" they said in unrehearsed unison, which of course, surprised Elizabeth.

"Well, Elizabeth, I knew you had the powers of persuasion," he complimented.

"Oh yes, they jumped on board immediately. No task too difficult for PCU," she said a bit perplexed look on her face.

"Well, goddesses, I'll let you enjoy Mount Olympus in peace. But, if you don't mind, I'll be contacting each one of you, you know, for a brief interview, just to get an idea on what achievements or happy memories you want presented in the piece."

"We look forward to it," Elizabeth smiled.

The three remained silent for a few moments as they watched the tight pairs of jeans fade away.

"Come back, Shane, come back," Tasha purred.

Chapter fifteen:

Horizon Lost?

As Dawn and Elizabeth headed home, Tasha reversed her direction, and headed west toward the famous *Lost Horizon* viewpoint.

Sitting in her car, she began to put together all the pieces that had been handed to her.

"Well, Miranda, let's see, the two pictures you sent me, the name of the Marlboro Man, the revelation that those Philistines, Elizabeth and Dawn, have been convinced that you are guilty. And, I'm somewhat sold on the theory that Mr. Wanna Be Hell's Angel is a key player in your production."

"Are you okay, Miss?"

For the second time in a matter of a few days, Tasha almost jumped out of the driver seat. Staring over at the tight jeans and shit eating grin, Tasha smiled. "Make that totally sold, Miranda."

"Sorry, didn't hear what you said," Roger said, no doubt knowing that words were their least important level of communication at that point.

"Said, you need to stop scaring me."

"Well, you need to stop...well, parking your car on the side of the road."

"So are you following me?"

"Quit flattering yourself, Babe. You're a gorgeous piece of scenery, but this view has you slightly beat," he said walking on over to the car. "They used it in *Lost Horizon* you know."

"Of course, I know. You like that movie?"

"Of course," he said inviting himself into the rented vette. "Sometimes we all need a Shangri-La. And for your two former roommates, I would say this weekend was theirs."

"And for me," Tasha said almost daring him to come on to her.

"Oh Tasha, I suspect you're the Prime Minister of Shangri-la. President of Elysian Fields. Mayor of Nirvana," he said slightly moving toward her.

"Still shows," she said moving toward him. She wasn't quite sure why she was playing this game at the moment, maybe because he seemed more interested in Elizabeth at the table. Oh, who said competition can be healthy.

"So, you going to take me on a sidetrip?" he asked.

Tasha was now a little nervous, not quite sure she meant for this seduction to happen, but when said he wanted to take a ride in mountains in the vette, she felt a strong sense of relief.

"Did I tell you I took a few stunt driving classes," Tasha teased as she put the foot strong to the metal.

"Isn't that a requirement for any Sam Cannon/Jacob Felding production?" he winked.

"So you're aware of some of my roles?" Tasha couldn't help but be flattered.

"And you're married to Felding. Probably one of the busiest TV directors of all time. I know he works for a lot of producers. But he struck gold, hooking up with Cannon."

"You know how they hooked up don't you," Tasha asked smugly.

"Folklore has it you were fucking them both," he said as he reached over and played with her hair. She smiled back as to confirm the rumor. "And."

"And, Tony Winters as well," she finished the sentence for him.

"The daytime soap creator. So you're pretty much responsible for one network's decade of high rating. Both nighttime and daytime."

"And the fuckers reward me by killing off my character."

"Renee loved you on that show. She hasn't watched it since."

"Renee is your..."

"Wife," he said.

Tasha was a bit disappointed in hearing that word. "She's one of your biggest fans. She made me promise to introduce you two."

That made Tasha feel a bit better.

"Maybe during your week on campus, I can hook the two of you up," Roger offered.

"The old going back home scenario. Wonder what moron in the Marketing Department came up with that overused cliché?" Tasha said with utter disrespect.

"Me."

"Oh fuck," Tasha swerved then tried to get the vette back on the main road. "Sorry, I didn't mean to belittle, you know what I mean. Are you employed by PCU?"

"I know. I know. And no," he laughed at her expense. "I'm a freelance guy with a camera and I offered my services to help make recruiting videos. Need to bring in some money, you know? And after a few short but well-received ones, I selfishly proposed this huge project. So far, so good."

Tasha glanced over at him, and decided to take the bait. "As Bing Crosby said to Rosemary Clooney in *White Christmas*, 'Everybody's got an angle.' So what's yours?"

"You."

"Excuse me."

"I wanted to meet you. Elizabeth and Dawn are the bonuses. But you are the prize."

"Well, yes I am. But why specifically do you think so?"

"Your ties, and I mean that in the bondage sense, with Cannon and Felding." he teased still playing with her hair.

Tasha looked at him half-pissed. "You want a job."

"A real, bonafied, money-making, just the break I need job."

"You think you can just jump in and direct a television show?"

He continued to play with her hair. "Hell, I'll start anywhere. I just want the employment and income of a season long show. Cannon's got enough of those lying around."

Tasha laughed in amazement. "I'm flattered. You obviously put a lot of thought and effort into this. I'm mean; I feel badly that I'm not the poker chip you think I am. I mean I can hardly get myself employed."

"But I doubt you've been bored or idle."

She looked over at him, sitting there quite smug with himself. Oh yes, he had agendas.

"I'll see what I can do."

"I promise more soft lighting for you than the other two."

"And you must say some incredibly nice things about me."

"Can't call you the vacuous nymph?"

"Wow," exclaimed Tasha, as she swerved again. They guy was ruining her concentration.

"Whoa, lady, stay on our side of the road."

"What the hell? "Why did you say that?"

"Vacuous nymph? I read it. In one of those now famous PCU editorials written by Kip Morgan, criticizing one Miranda Taylor of her many liberal stands, this time taking pot shots at some of her supporters, such as her roommates."

"Yeah, as if he actually wrote it. Like he would know what vacuous meant."

"True, that's why it is so strange that Miranda let him get to her. Why she would feel so threatened? Why would she feel a need to put a stop to his ranting?"

With each word, Tasha accelerated even more, and with a few seconds was very close to going off the road and into some tree."

"Whoa, Sally," he said attempting to sound calm, "Got to slow your Mustang down."

"This is not a piece of shit Mustang. It is a Corvette," Tasha yelled.

"I think I hit a nerve. Should we go with it?"

"Go? You want to go with something, buddy boy? Go with this." And she pressed the gas pedal with full force causing the car to squeal and swerve. One year, her stunt driving instructor had praised her natural abilities however; she never finished the advanced class. Roger grabbed the steering wheel, kicked her foot out of the way, and somehow, no doubt with the assistance of some divine intervention, managed to take control of the car and safely get them to a view point where they sat hyperventilating.

"Philistine," she growled. "I was doing fine." And then she began crying.

"You're one mercurial brat."

"I nearly killed us and that's your response?"

"Listen, obviously we conjured up some evil spirits within each other. Can we just rest here and restore the good vibes that had been developing?"

She nodded. "I would like that," she sniffed and recovered.

Roger then jumped out of the car and walked around the vette. Opening her door, and taking her hand, he led her to a huge stone and sat up against it with his legs extended and straddled. He then placed her back up against him and began playing with her hair again.

"I guess I was out of line," he apologized. "I mean, of course the subject of Miranda murdering Kip has got to be quite painful for you."

"Allegedly murdering Kip," she corrected. "She was just a suspect."

"Honey, she was the only suspect, and quite frankly, she still is a suspect."

"According to Topanga's finest. But then, they didn't exactly make a great effort to figure out the truth."

"What was there to figure out? She lured him out there with this bogus tale of a cheating ring. Lost her cool in an argument and drew a knife. Do you have a better scenario?"

She tensed up a bit. "No, but I mean, it's not up to me to provide one. Hell, I wasn't out there. No one but Kip and Miranda."

"And Ricky and Larry."

"Those fucking clowns."

"Those fucking clowns provided damaging evidence against your roommate. I mean, they were the only eyewitnesses to the crime."

"Fuck it. There's not much you and I can do about it anyway. Can we just sit here and relax."

"Only if you let me play with your hair and make you weak."

She definitely envied his wife. A man with such a sensuous touch was hard to find. He had natural talent that had been augmented with classic training in the fine art of massage. She was not sure if it was a few minutes or twenty, but hands gradually worked their way down to her neck and shoulders, and then even lower to her back and around her waist.

"The hell with the spa, I should just schedule my sessions with you," she joked after 30 minutes of pure bliss.

"You help me get a job with Cannon, and I'll massage you all you want."

She turned around and placed her lips very close to his. "I can get a fabulous massage in four different states if I wanted to."

Roger smiled and placed his arms around her tightly. "So goddess, what's a poor starving artist to do then?"

"I don't know, you sweet little Satyr, but I'm sure I'll figure out a task for you at some point."

"And then?"

"And then, I'll bestow my blessings upon you. But remember, Paris got Helen and look at what a disaster that was."

"Yeah, but what a legend it created," he said as he gently kissed her on the lips before escorting her back to the car.

"You want to drive?" she asked him.

"Well, sure, but I'm somewhat surprised you would let me."

"If and when you start working for Cannon, and you run into my husband, you will not mention this. Or a lot of other things, too."

"And the same rule applies when you meet Renee. Agree?"

Tasha smiled and nodded. She loved sharing secrets with men. In fact, she was downright addicted to it. When they reached his cycle at the viewpoint, Roger stroked her cheek before taking off down the mountain.

"Fade-out," Tasha laughed.

Chapter sixteen:

The Marlboro Man

It took a few phone calls on Tuesday morning, but within hours, Tasha had located one Jack Schwartz in the nearby city of Hemet, where he was enjoying retirement and helping to manage the local riding stable.

On Wednesday morning, the old genuine Levi 501 jeans hugged Kasha's hips. She moaned while looking in the full-length mirror in her walk-in closet. Jeans were not the most flattering attire for her hour glass figure, with special emphasis on the later hours; but, if she was going to snag an old cowpoke, she had better not be seen in designer jeans. Completing the outfit with genuine black leather boots, genuine black leather hat with genuine snakeskin trim, and a form-fitting red shirt that tied at the waist, she resembled a genuine horse-loving cowgirl. Now she would just have to fake it for a few hours.

With the help of the Thomas Brothers, she had no trouble finding the stable, where a lovely gentle mustang by the name of Moonshine awaited her. As she mounted the equine, she saw a white Ford Explorer pull up, and it was her guess that rugged man sitting inside was none other than Jack Schwartz.

Tasha and Moonshine trotted around a bit as Jack groomed and prepared his horse. When he started off for his daily ride, she caught up with him.

"Excuse me! Excuse me, sir. Would it be okay if I rode with you a bit? I'm not familiar with the trails here."

He looked at her and regarded her for a moment. She could tell that he found her attractive, and eerily familiar. "Well, miss, you strike me as an intelligent and resourceful woman, and the trails here are clearly marked. I'm sure you will do just fine without me."

"But my guess is you know some of the more out of the way, interesting trails."

"And my guess is you can find anything that is out of the way and interesting on your own. You're an experienced rider, I can tell."

"Yes, sir. I have been riding since college."

"Well, now I pegged you for an intelligent woman didn't I?" He rode off.

She hollered, "I was taught by my roommate." But Tasha could tell he was ignoring her. Feeling desperate, she gave it one last try. "Her name was Dawn Wolfe." That caught his attention and he returned, which Tasha mentally chalked up as a victory.

"So, your roommate taught you, huh. Did you graduate from a local university?"

"Sort of. Parnassus Canyon University in Topanga. Class of 1973."

Within seconds his faced possessed a devilish grin that nearly surpassed the width of his face.

"So, you're the Goldberg girl. Thought I recognized you. You're even prettier now. And of course, even prettier in person."

"So, you've seen some of my work?" the actress in her couldn't help asking.

"A little. My wife watched that damn soap of yours. Was miffed as hell when they killed you off."

Tasha was beginning to wonder if she should approach the producers with the wrong body-amnesia concept.

"So are you the Marlboro Man?" she said keeping her priorities straight.

He looked at her questioningly for a few moments. When he still didn't respond, Tasha whipped out the old cigarette box and handed it to him.

"That is my handwriting, miss," he acknowledged.

"So you are the Marlboro Man."

"Well, Miss, I guess I am. Are you Glipsa?"

"Glipsa?" her vocal inflection surprised her and almost threatened any rapport that had developed with the horseman. "No, I'm not," she said in a hurry, "but I know who and what she is. She is a rag doll. Dawn's rag doll. Why do you ask?"

He didn't answer, but instead studied her for what seemed like an incredibly long time; but Tasha, feeling in the driver seat, and used to public recognition, allowed him to take all the time he needed. "So, did I tell you, there are some wonderful trails on the other side of that hill?" he asked, finally breaking the silence. "Care to join me?"

"Would love to."

Over on the other side, Jack and Tasha engaged in small talk for about an hour. She learned about his retirement, his late wife, his daughters and their families that lived nearby. While he was a charming storyteller, and she was not bored, she had not driven a few hours, much less stuffed her hips into an unflattering article of clothing, for this kind of discourse.

"So, why are you here?" he finally asked.

Even though her head was full of questions, ideas, and theories, she found herself unable to formulate or articulate a cohesive sentence. After a few feeble attempts, the lone cowboy came to her rescue.

"You want to know more about the case."

Now why couldn't she think of something that simple?

"Why?" he asked.

"Well," she answered, "she was my roommate and my friend."

"Funny. I never figured you two had a lot in common."

"I never claimed we were soul mates."

"It's been nearly twenty years. Why now?"

"Twenty year reunion coming up. Mid-life crisis. I don't really know, other than it seemed the thing to do."

"Well, as you know, the Taylor girl had written a series of articles, exposing years of corruption within our department. Well, I was one of her sources. Probably the main source."

"You helped her score her biggest triumph. She was damn proud of those pieces.

And as I recalled, some heads rolled afterwards."

"Yes, they did, and it was long overdue. Now after the articles were printed, she contacted me again, and told me she was investigating the practice of gang raping on campus. Said it would involve some important names."

"Kip Morgan?"

"She did not name names at that time, but said something about some great pieces of evidence she had obtained. I told her to be careful with them, and she something about them being safe with Glipsa. We agreed to meet the following week. But a few days later, well, you know the rest."

"I take it you never did find that evidence."

"That's right. He then pulled her horse closer to his and whispered, "But I did get some evidence of that poor fool's accident. It wasn't murder, you know."

Tasha's heart started pounding and she had s throng desire to kiss him. "I didn't think it was murder." Then she presented her best devilish smile, "So, you gonna spill or what?"

"Miss, I would prefer you not resort to B detective movies lingo. But, of course, I'll share what I know," he said emphasizing the last sentence. "I was in the dark in the parking lot, trying to figure out some things in this difficult case I was working on, when I saw Degas, and one of his kiss-ass protégés come out to talk. Well, I knew they were speaking out there for a reason, so I snuck to where I could overhear them."

"What did you hear?"

"That John Morgan had called him on his direct line. Apparently his son and the Taylor girl had had some sort of altercation and the boy was now dead. John was going to need a few hours and then he would call the station. Degas wanted that brown noser to be on the phones and to make sure that call went to Degas and to nobody else."

"Did John Morgan have that kind of clout at your station?"

"Let me just say, I think his annual budget for our services was almost as much as the county's. And he obviously had friends in even higher places, because he didn't fall with the rank and file."

"What happened next?"

"Well, at that point, I drove on over to the crime scene."

"What did you find?"

"I was lucky in that his two friends had left already, so I took a good look at the body and took a few Polaroid's."

"You did?" Tasha screeched. "Did you ever turn those pictures in?"

"No, I didn't."

"But why?"

"Well, it was obvious that there was going to be a conspiracy, involving many members of the department. And you see, any acts that went against the conspiracy would be treated and punished as treason. Besides, if you let your prey know that you're on their trail, they only know that they have to cover their tracks better or perhaps even leave an ambush for you."

"Why didn't you just hand them over to her mother's attorney?"

"He would have had an obligation to share them and I was worried that the pictures would end up just like the knife. Plus, I figured if Miranda didn't return, then she really didn't have confidence in this attorney and I shouldn't either."

"What do you mean, end up like the knife?"

"Got lost."

"Lost! When and how?"

"Well, as you recall, the Taylor girl was considered a murder suspect who crossed over state lines. Well, that brought in the FBI. Now, I know full well, that they had their doubts about the murder case, too, but let's face it; they had their own private agenda. By playing along, they were able to get the green light to obtain warrants and search her room and her belonging, plus homes and offices of friends and family members. They were even allowed to set up surveillances. You know they even caught up with a few old, shall we say, friends. And some of these old friends had drugs, or weapons or something on them. Yeah, the feds were happy with the whole situation. They didn't care if the Taylor girl was ever found."

Tasha knew that was the last thing Miranda wanted.

"Well, with the evidence going back and forth between police, FBI, and the different attorneys, it was only a matter of time before something got lost."

"Do you think, the knife had some help in getting lost?"

"Of course it did. Miranda's fingerprints were nowhere to be seen on that knife. Plus, the knife, the one she supposedly owned and used; well, it was engraved, in gold no less, with a number 67 on it. Now, I don't know too much about Miranda Taylor, but she did not strike me as one who would wear earrings, much less get her weapons engraved. And the number 67, wasn't that the number Kip wore on his football jersey?"

Jack wiped his forehead and laughed. "You know the theory that she had obtained that switchblade from some subversive organization? Well, come on, just how much business do you think took place between Tijuana vendors and the Weathermen? Or the Black Panthers? Most extremist opted for more lethal weapons and tried to keep them basically generic."

Tasha laughed, too, finding him more and more endearing.

"Yeah, only a self-centered brat, like Kip Morgan, would think of engraving a switchblade," he said.

"Whatever happened to Degas?"

"Quit the department shortly after the Kip Morgan case. Last I heard, he had his own security company, catering to the rich and famous."

"Doesn't seem fair. He came out smelling like a rose."

"Well, now he has access to certain social circles and plenty of material possessions. I guess that's important to him. But you know a man like John Morgan reminds me of MacBeth. Now, I know you're surprised that some old weathered sheriff like me can name a character from Shakespeare."

"My guess is that there are a lot of things about you that would surprise me."

"Too bad you never got deputized," he smiled. "Men like John Morgan get to where they get by squashing if not eliminating anything or anyone in their way. So it is only natural that they become suspicious of their subordinates. Men like John Morgan protect themselves by building a strong fortress around them and some of the bricks are made from undying loyalties from the inner circles. Now if someone's loyalty is in question, his fate is usually determined in the bottom of the moat. My guess is that Anthony Degas has taken his share of swimming lessons, but still panics whenever he sees a cement mixer around."

Tasha laughed at that image. "You don't think Degas could bring Morgan down?"

"Only if he desired to be a Kamikaze pilot. He's done too much to remain unscathed. At best, he can hope that Morgan decides not to toss him over into the moat. You see, miss, I may not live in a fancy mansion, or escort movies stars to their seats; but, look at all this," he said indicating the whole valley in which they were riding. "I wake up each morning knowing I did my best for the public. Then I spend some time here with my horse, Decker, eat some lunch. Say, would you care to join me for lunch? It's just over the hill. I guarantee you the juiciest hamburgers you'll ever taste and pool tables in tip top shape."

"I would love to, Jack."

As they began to head off, Tasha inquired, "Any chance that I can see the pictures?"

"Now what makes you think I still have them?"

"And the knife?"

"Damn, it is a shame that you were never deputized. Any good at pool?"

"Graduated from PCU, didn't I?"

Tasha immediately fell in love with the Triple D Bar & Grill. It reminded her some of the more interesting men in her life—void of any charm or health codes.

"I guess the ambiance is a little different than what you're used to," Jack said as she waited for her eyes to adjust to the darkness.

"Well, I have lived a varied life. Don't worry; I can handle a place like this."

"I know. And that's what scares me."

Jack's status was rather high in this place, securing them a pool table right away.

Tasha had honed her skills in lieu of studying many a night at PCU. But after a few games, it was pitifully apparent that the police academies provided better pool-playing curriculum.

"So," he said walking up behind her. "You want to take a look at something you think I might have."

"You know I do."

"Well, that's a pretty nasty shot there waiting for you. You sink it in on the next shot and I just might feel nostalgic."

Jacked waltzed over to the other side as Tasha tried to remember everything she could about geometrical shapes and positioning of the stick, then, the hell with it, she decided to leave it to the fates as she shoved the cue stick into the white ball. Watching the four ball roll toward its destination, she began a little prayer of thanks, only to be appalled by the sick humor of the three sisters when the ball ended up bouncing off the pocket and landing a mere four inches from the hole.

She was about to curse out loud when she saw Jack, who had turned away to pay the waitress, use his right hand to achieve illegally what she and the fates could not.

"I'm glad we're on the same side," she said as he took her arm to escort her outside.

Jack then took her to the stable's back office and pulled out a hidden safe.

"I'm surprised you don't have a safe deposit box."

"Professional criminals know how to get into them. And remember, in our line of work, we meet many professionals on a daily basis." He started to hand the pictures to her then quickly retreated. "They are rather gruesome. I suggest you look take a quick glance at just one." Tasha utilized her improvisational skills to react as if she hadn't a clue how Kip looked as he met his maker."

"And here is the knife. And something even more special, the original forensics report."

Tasha took a look at it, and was not surprised to see the mention of alcohol and marijuana in his system. "What about the newspaper story, that said he was clean."

"Easy. Somebody anonymously leaked the no-substance found in the body statement to the press, and the press went with it. The department refused to comment, and so, by default, that story became the official story. As for the report that is now in the file, well, some flunky probably earned an early retirement. Everybody has a price, you know."

"But wouldn't the medical examiner expose that during the trial?"

"Miss, there was never going to be a trial. Trust me, there's a reason why Miranda ran, and I kept these hidden for all these years."

"The pictures. I can understand you having them, but how did you get those sturdy paws on the knife and forensics report?"

"They were retrieved from Anthony Degas's safe deposit box."

"You didn't?"

"Of course, I didn't. I just said it happened."

"So, those bank boxes."

"Now, don't worry. I'm sure your silver and your wills are perfectly safe. But nothing is foolproof to a professional."

"And you meet professionals on a daily basis."

He nodded.

"So, in a nutshell, you gathered all this great evidence? What were you going to do with it?"

"Wait for someone to come hunting for it. It was too a good a case to remain dormant. Had all the classic elements. I knew eventually someone would take a second look at that case, and they would find me. Although, I never guessed it would be you."

"Me either. But I've learned not to second guess the fates a long time ago."

"So now, what are you going to do with them," he asked.

"Exonerate Miranda."

"That's a pretty big job you're taking on."

"I'll have some divine intervention. And don't worry; I won't reveal your assistance."

"Miss, I don't care if you do. I know I withheld and stole evidence, but I think history will show that I was not the one obstructing justice. I would be willing to talk now."

"Morgan is still pretty powerful."

Schwartz looked at her longingly. "And I will be joining my wife soon. I think it would be nice to join her with a totally clear conscious."

"I'm sorry," she said stroking his arm. She looked at his rugged face that feared no death, but wanted just one last bit of pleasure on this earth. Tasha didn't even have to act when she allowed him to passionately kiss her.

Chapter seventeen:

The Golden Fleece

"Good morning, goddess, just calling to make sure you got home okay, and really to see if Dawn had more to say on the drive back to Marin," Tasha said that Thursday morning.

"Thanks, goddess. Yes, I'm fine, although I sometimes wonder how the whole legal world can function without me. My God, on Tuesday, I needed a crane to get all the stuff off my desk. Not that I'm complaining. One more good settlement and it's skiing in the Alps."

Tasha didn't dare remind Elizabeth that while she did indeed earn great money to pay for some fabulous vacations, between her and her husband's workaholic tendencies, the kids usually went with a nanny while parents stayed home and worked some more.

"Yes, all those revelations about Dawn were quite surprising. Just never expected the calm, analytical one to face burn out," Elizabeth said.

"Can you handle another surprise?" Tasha asked seriously.

"Oh, not you and Jacob?"

"No, I know no one expects us to last. It's only been eleven years," she said with a hint of sarcasm. "But seriously, sit down, because last night I received a call from a friend who used to write for one of those real crime shows. And he was preparing a piece on Kip's death"

"Oh shit, please tell me it's not going to air during our reunion."

"It's not going to air at all. He quit that project."

"Why?"

"He became convinced that she didn't do it."

"Oh Tasha, we just had this debate," she said with some irritation in her voice.

"Listen, I think that's a clue for you to recheck everything."

"Tasha, I did once, and I wasn't happy with what I found," Elizabeth said losing her patience with the whole subject.

"So look again," she started to beg, which she hated to do.

"Now, Tasha, don't take this the wrong way," which always meant Tasha would, "but you are describing the perfect movie of the week for yourself. And I hope you get a great part. But I have at least 80 billable hours still waiting for me on my desk. I haven't even checked my voicemail this morning."

"But."

"Tasha, God love you for your idealism and alternative thinking. But, for the most part, I have to deal with reality," Elizabeth said sternly before hanging up.

Well, that didn't go well, Tasha thought. Plan B. Call Dawn.

"Thanks for calling, Tasha, I just hope I didn't give you and Elizabeth the wrong impression, I really am okay."

"We know you are, and I'm thankful you can vent with me."

"You have always been a good friend. A friend that has gotten me into more than my fair share of trouble, but a true friend."

"Well, thanks. Love you, too. And in this moment of sentiment, I need to ask you a favor. You know how those things fell out of your scrapbook?"

"Yes, that was strange, wasn't it?"

"Well, I can't help but wonder if there isn't more. I mean Miranda kept copious notes and she had a ton of secret sources. None of that information was ever discovered."

"Maybe she took them with her. When she took my VW," she said with years of disappointment in her voice.

Ouch, Tasha thought to herself. "Or maybe she hid them quite well. Maybe in some of your other stuff."

"Like what?"

"I don't know. Old record covers. Jewelry boxes. Glipsa."

"Glipsa? Tasha, are you auditioning for a role of another murderess?"

"Dawn, I know it all sounds so..."

"Dramatic? Yes it does, Tasha, and I know how you don't want to believe that Miranda could commit such a heinous act, but at some point, you are going to have to deal with it. Please let me give you a name of someone in your area."

"Dawn, I don't want to speak to a therapist," Tasha shot back.

"Listen, Tasha, I'll get that name for you later. I'm running late and I have a staff meeting in just a few minutes. Shit, we lost another grant, but that's my dilemma, not yours," she said before hanging up.

"Well, that sucked even more." Tasha said hanging up.

"Plan C anyone?"

The next morning, Tasha put plan C in action. Dressed in a bright red power suit, Victoria Secret Lingerie underneath, five-inch black heels, and her hair loosely pinned with curls naughtily dangling, she left her house for a day of taking no live prisoners.

Tasha walked into Roger's Santa Monica office and found him, dressed in jeans and a Van Halen t-shirt, in front of a monitor, viewing what appeared to be an awful industrial film, and pushing all sorts of buttons, dealing with the dialogue tract. She may have been forced to take some technology classes while earning her Theatre Arts degree, but that didn't mean she had to actually learn anything.

"Christ, the acting is scary," she said as he pulled her down onto his lap.

"But it pays the bills," he said. "You look gorgeous, if not overpowering today. Going to conduct a hostile take over?"

"Sort of," she said stroking his face. "I want to share something with you. And get that excited look off your face," she laughed as she presented all the evidence Jack Schwartz had given her. She didn't have to worry, thought because within a few seconds that look was replaced with a stunned, almost horrified expression.

"I...I..." he stammered, totally incapable of formulating any words.

"I know, that's okay, dear," she said as she pulled him to her bosom to comfort him.

"This...this..."

"Conflicts with the official story."

"Mother fuck, what are you doing with this? How the hell did you get this stuff," he asked somewhat shocked.

"It's amazing how brave some people get when they're near death."

"Who else knows?"

"The source, you and me."

"So not Elizabeth and Dawn?"

"No. And for right now, I need to keep it that way." Tasha then took his face gently in her hands. "But I also need information that only they can provide."

"Well, how are you going to ask them?" he wondered.

"I'm not. You are," she told him.

"Me?"

"Yes, dear. When you call Elizabeth and Dawn for their interviews, say nothing about what I have shown you or our conversations. I want you to casually bring up Miranda and just mention how there has been some recent rumors regarding a conspiracy to frame Miranda. And just also mention possible movies being made and you being a possible director." She kissed his forehead. "Think you can do that for me, dear?"

"I can. But I can't help wondering why don't you just tell them what you know and ask them for the information yourself?"

"Oh my dear, that would be the upfront and honest approach. It's never been my style."

Roger placed his arms around her waist and kissed her on the neck. "You can't help being who you are, can you?

"No, I can't." Tasha stood up and kissed him lightly on the lips before heading to the door. She would have loved to stay all day and play, but her theatre training had taught her that an exit is just as important as an entrance.

"So, what are you piloting today," he asked as he leaned back in his chair.

"Just the Beemer." She smiled and turned to walk away. As she opened the door, he called out, "Hey."

"Yes?"

"If I get the Golden Fleece for you. What do I get?"

"An introduction to Sam Cannon."

That made his day.

Chapter eighteen:

Picking up the Pieces

It was almost a week later when Tasha received the expected, but still frantic call from Elizabeth at her office.

"Tasha, we have some things to discuss. Get yourself in a private spot."

Elizabeth in general mode, thought Tasha, that's got to be a good sign.

"Tasha, I was thinking that it was strange how Larry and Ricky didn't show up for 10 year reunion, especially since they still live in L.A. and are quite successful. And also, since John Morgan is still on the Board and still a big football booster."

Tasha could have been upset that Elizabeth was claiming these thoughts as her own, but considering the circumstances, she was going to let it go.

"So I decided to check into the case against Miranda again."

"Good idea," Tasha said ironically.

"It sure was." Elizabeth took a deep breath. "Bottom line is that since graduation, one of the main witnesses, Larry Davidson, has worked exclusively for John Morgan in one capacity or another. His beautiful lifestyle has been totally financed by Morgan. His gorgeous home is actually owned by the company. His cars are leased through the company. And even his beautiful, great hostess wife, a former Miss Orange County, is a former play thing of John Morgan."

"That's weird," Tasha acknowledged. "However, the argument could be made that he's just helping out an old friend of his son," Tasha said imitating Elizabeth.

"True. But he also helped out Ricky Zogobo, in the same manner, except he married a former Miss Sacramento."

"Once again, he was a good friend of the beloved deceased son," Tasha just couldn't help herself.

"Yes, but this little piggy could not recognize a good thing when he had one. First of all, Ricky was stupid enough to embezzle money, get arrested for spousal abuse and apparently never met a gram of coke he didn't like. But his *coup de grace* was bragging that he never had to worry because John Morgan was afraid of him, and what he knew."

"I've been in enough thrillers to know that one does not advertise such information. I can't imagine he got away with that for too long."

"No dear, he didn't. He was forgiven for the taking of money. All criminal charges against him were dropped. But, I guess, bragging is an unforgivable sin. A few years ago, he was transferred to a position in Borrego Springs, where he died of a drug overdose within a few weeks."

Tasha gasped and held her hand to her heart, hoping to slow down the beat. "You don't think?" Tasha said in disbelief.

"Widow and children are still doing fine. Very well taken care of."

"Elizabeth, it almost sounds as if."

"Oh, I know. And just for the record, Anthony Degas, lead detective on the case, now has his own security company, financed by Morgan. But don't worry about his lifestyle—he's sitting pretty in both house and car—courtesy of Sugar Daddy of the Year, John Morgan.

That old cowboy was right, thought Tasha.

"Tasha, John Morgan was a family friend. He and my father did quite a bit of business together. It just sickens me. But, you know there is something even worse," Elizabeth said obviously somewhat pained.

"Oh my, god, what?"

Elizabeth started to speak and then stopped abruptly to clear her throat, suggesting that she was fighting back the tears. Tasha could feel the butterflies inside of her going ballistic, because Elizabeth hardly ever cried.

"I don't know if you recall this, but according to Ricky and Larry's statement, they went looking for Kip around ten that night and when they found him murdered, they drove to the Community Volunteer Center and called John Morgan."

"Sounds vaguely familiar."

"Jesus Christ, Tasha," Elizabeth said in a self-berating manner, "that center closed at nine. There is no way possible they could have made the call in that center at that time. So either, they called from another spot, or at another time. But either way, they lied about the time of death. And witnesses usually do not lie about the time of death, unless they are hiding something."

"That's good Elizabeth, that's a gem of a find," Tasha said, not quite sure why Elizabeth was still so upset.

"Tasha, yes it's significant and it changes a lot of things. But don't you see, the fucking ASB, of which I was the president, not only started the center, but ran it, and there wasn't anything about it that I didn't know, including what time it shut it's doors. If I had caught that our senior year, I could have alerted someone. Things could have turned out differently. And most of all," she said sobbed.

"What, honey?" Tasha said, adding her own tears.

"I could have gone all these years not thinking that Miranda was guilty. I let her down, Tasha."

Boy, there is a stiff penalty for being such a perfectionist, Tasha thought to herself, and Elizabeth's self-loathing was not going to make Tasha's next step even easier.

"Elizabeth, do you have tangible proof of what you've told me. Contracts, maybe deeds?"

"Yes, why?"

"Can you overnight me copies. I would like to present it to that producer I was telling you about. But I want to control what is presented and how."

"Sure, it's the least I can do for Miranda right now. Is that the same film that Roger might be working on?"

Tasha smiled to herself for a job well done. "Yes, I've heard that rumor, too. But producers have been known to string a couple of directors along, so we better not say too much to Roger at the reunion, okay." Tasha said, hoping to keep Roger more to herself.

"You're right. I guess it is a blessing that he left two days ago or I probably would have handed everything over to him."

"Left? Left where?" Tasha wanted to know.

"Marin County. He hopped on his bike and headed south."

"He was in Marin County?"

"Yes, for the interview. Remember he said he was going to contact us. Well, the rebel just showed up on Monday."

"I tried calling you at the office that day, and your secretary said you would be at a meeting all day."

"In a sense, I was."

Tasha could feel Elizabeth blush in girlish delight and Tasha tried not to exude her steam over the phone. "Got on the bike?"

"All the way to San Francisco, for lunch in some biker's bar. Me in a white suit."

"Well, Muffy and Penelope would be proud," Tasha teased, camouflaging her jealousy.

"I think they would. Tasha, this producer friend of yours."

"Everything is confidential. Don't worry."

After hanging up, Tasha felt good about what had been accomplished Miranda-wise; but felt Roger's agenda would require some checking into.

"Shit," Tasha yelled jumping a few inches into the air as the phone rang.

"Tasha, I've made some uncomfortable revelation which we need to discuss. You might want to position yourself in a place where you can think and react naturally." Dawn was repeating Elizabeth's greeting, but in a more nurturing, less demanding fashion.

"What is it?"

"I opened Glipsa and made a disturbing discovery. Glipsa has been harboring, for who knows how long, a plastic bag full of panties with dates and initials written on them in felt pen. Plus a copy of a cashier check from the school to Ethan Borgheses for $25,000."

"Who's Ethan?" Tasha said, although the last name rang a bell.

"His daughter, Stephanie, was a freshman cheerleader our junior year."

"That's how I know the name. But didn't she get sick and leave school right before winter break?"

"The yearbook mentions a replacement for the winter sports. But on the back of the check, Miranda wrote down a few names, all classmates of ours at PCU."

"And?"

"I called one of them. Told him, I was calling for reunion committee."

"That's good."

"I've learned how to lie well from you, Tasha," Dawn said, almost bragging about her new skill.

"Thank you. And what happened?"

"Oh my God, Tasha. We were on the phone for a few hours. I won't bore you with all the superficial stuff, but in summary, this person told me that Kip and some of his friends made a practice of targeting pretty young women on campus, getting them drunk, and then gang-raping them. And to add to the sport, they would keep the panties, and marked the dates and the initials in felt pen. They were then kept on a laundry line in Kip's room and each time one was added, there was some sort of ritual. It's just too disturbing."

"Shit, I knew a lot of those guys in that dorm."

"You know, Tasha, he mentioned you specifically and how you were not considered an appropriate target."

"Let's face it, Dawn, I was probably too experienced and not a big enough challenge for that sick game."

"Well, historically virgins have always been considered the most valuable conquests."

Tasha took a deep breath, who knew her brazen personality actually saved her from a calamity for once. "And what about the check?"

"Stephanie was targeted one night. After they were through, she broke down, right there in the dorm. Apparently, she ran out naked into the main lobby, screaming and yelling. The head resident came out and immediately called security. She was taken away in an ambulance."

"I swear, I don't remember anything like that."

"It was kept quiet. The sheriffs intervened at the hospital and no sexual assault tests were taken. And to add insult to injury, she was diagnosed and treated as an alcohol and drug overdose. Later, she was given a stern warning and placed on probation by the school. The head resident was threatened with dismissal if he didn't gain control over the so-called drug problem in his dorm. And the culprits, well, they were told, unofficially, to be more careful."

"He told you all that, Dawn?"

"He's been living with that secret for years. Once he started, he couldn't stop talking. Secrets of that magnitude usually create all sorts of new issues."

"Don't I know," Tasha said softly to herself. "Say, Dawn. I know this sounds strange, but this revelation is making a few memories a bit clearer. Do you suppose, I could see that stuff? I mean, would you feel okay shipping everything to me."

"That or I could just give it to Roger. He mentioned the Hollywood research that is going on, so I don't suppose it would a problem for him to have possession for a day."

"Roger?" Tasha asked.

"Yes, you know the filmmaker, we met him in Ojai."

"Sure, I remember, I just didn't remember him going to Phoenix."

"Sure you do. Remember for the interview."

Tasha could have sworn he said he would be calling them, as in telephone.

"Well, that would be okay, if he has room on his bike."

"What bike?" Dawn inquired.

"His motorcycle," Tasha almost yelled somewhat frustrated.

"Oh, he didn't' bring it, Tasha," Dawn said with an excitement that hadn't been heard in years in her voice. "He drove a white Jaguar." Then Tasha could hear Dawn giggle, another rare noise from her, "I've never been in a white Jaguar."

"Wow. A Jaguar, dirty jeans and all."

"Actually, we must have met him on a day off, because he was dressed in a beautiful light grey suit, blue shirt, and even a tie."

"Lunch?" she said not knowing if she really wanted an answer.

"He treated me at the Pointe. I have never been there. Tasha, it was a great day."

If it were anyone else, Tasha would have accused the person of deliberate torture, but sweet Dawn hadn't a clue how she was taking a hammer to Tasha's head. The only thing saving her sanity at the moment was the knowledge that she would have to pick up the items from Roger. And then she would find out what's going on with that naughty Satyr.

Chapter nineteen:

Seducing Roger

Roger had seen her flower child side in Ojai, her corporate witch side at his office and now she would tease him in her bikini with open jacket when he dropped off Dawn's findings.

"Those are real, right?" Roger said carrying a small box in.

"Absolutely!"

"And hair color and the nails?" he wiggled his eyebrows.

"Sweet cheeks, I pay hard cold cash for these nails. They're mine. Just try to take them," she challenged.

"When I take you, I'll take a hell of a lot more than just nails," he said kissing her hand.

"You seem confident that you are safe with that kind of behavior. You're assuming that Jacob or children are not here."

"It's daylight, honey. Chances are kids are at school and Jacob is on one set or another. Plus, you were specific about what time I had to come by."

Tasha felt a bit busted.

"I can only assume you're being somewhat secretive about all this information you are gathering."

"I am," she said as she took the box and carried it into one of the spare bedrooms that functioned as her office.

"So," he said, following her in. "When do I meet the famous and oh so productive Sam Cannon?"

"Soon." Tasha turned and looked at him. She could see he was feeling somewhat conned. "Okay, honey, I know I'm not known for my integrity, but I will get you an introduction. Come here," she said indicating the couch. "I'll start planting the seeds now, and by the time the reunion is over and you're done with that rah-rah PCU project, you'll be set to go." She took his hands, and massaged them gently. "Now, I can get you a mere introduction, or I can pretty much guarantee a job."

"And what other Herculean Task will be required of me?"

"When the reunion is over and I have had time to sift through all this evidence, I want you to make a documentary on the case. One of those award-winning documentaries that get college students and liberals all upset and on the bandwagon. And I will finance it. But that must be kept secret."

"We are going to have our share of secrets, aren't we, doll?"

"And that will bring us so much closer," she whispered.

"I bet," he winked at her.

"So, rumor has it you took Elizabeth to a biker bar for lunch. And Dawn, to the exquisite Pointe."

"How do these rumors get started," he moved closer, ran his fingers through her hair.

"Most men wouldn't dare to think about putting Elizabeth, in a Chanel suit with matching pumps, on the back of a Harley. Or, practical, down to earth Dawn in a Jaguar."

"Honey, I would think you of all people, would appreciate the jumping outside the box," he said as he feathered his fingers down her neck to her exposed breasts.

"But you knew exactly where to jump with both of them."

"Educated guesses."

Somehow Tasha didn't believe that, but she knew he wasn't going to reveal anything now, so she decided to be still and allow his hands to maneuver her down onto the couch, unclothed her and massaged her for two full hours.

After the massage, she offered to return the favor sometime.

"Maybe when we get together for your interview," he suggested.

"And that would be?" she asked.

"Don't get mad, but I'm pretty booked until the actual week of the reunion. You couldn't sneak away for a few hours or so, could you?"

Tasha thought for a moment. "I know Elizabeth will have to spend one night with her snooty parents in Beverly Hills. And Dawn, she's so professional, that she couldn't justify taking off a week without scheduling a training session at some LA Teen Hotline. I'll find out when those nights are and get in touch."

He reached over and hugged her, "Perfect. And by the way, I'm not expecting, you know the massage, to go any further."

"Don't worry, babe, it won't"

"Well, gee, you didn't have to be so sure about it. I mean, let me dream of a chance or something. And what makes you so sure?"

Tasha laughed. "You poor Satyr. Unfortunately you give such great massages; you've become way too valuable in that area. I have no trouble finding men who want to fuck me. But a good masseur is truly hard to find."

"Why can't a man be both?"

"Because, once he graduates to becoming a fucker, he loses interest in being a masseur. Trust me, I speak from experience," she said hugging him closely and kissing him on the cheek.

Tasha waved and watched him drive away from the curb. "Fade out," she giggled.

Chapter twenty:

Back to School

Bright and early on the first Monday in November, after being greeted by the current president, ASB officers, cheerleaders, and the local press, the famed PCU trio scurried up the stairs to their old room and quickly unpacked.

"Is it just me?" asked Tasha, "or have our tastes matured and refined over the years? I mean, was this room always this small and depressing?"

"I'm beginning to understand why my mother was so appalled that first day," added Elizabeth.

"And the president," Tasha interrupted. "Isn't he a bit young to be president? Aren't they suppose to be old men? Like when we were here?"

"Tasha, Ed Riley is the same exact age as President Luther was when we were here," Elizabeth informed her.

"Shit, now I really am depressed. You know, I have an idea."

"Oh shit," the other two said in unison.

"Knock it off, this is for real."

"That's what we're afraid of," answered Elizabeth.

"Let's go to the bathroom and see if it's still a hellhole."

"Oh yeah, that is going to brighten my day," Dawn commented sarcastically.

"Come on, Dawn, you know we're going to have to face that bathroom sometime this week," Elizabeth said, dragging her by the arm down the hall.

"I don't believe this," Elizabeth said as she pushed the back wall of the linen cabinet. "Everything is still the same."

"Our note," said Tasha. "You mean to tell me that not one student in the last two decades had the initiative to check and see if there was hiding place in here? No wonder our economy is failing."

"Or maybe, they never felt the need to hide and sneak around as much as you did," Dawn teased.

"True. You're either born with it or not. But still you would think the idea of a semester's worth of textbooks would have entered someone's sub-conscious," Tasha reasoned.

"Well, they're going to be redoing this floor soon," lamented Elizabeth. "It's a good chance that this whole cabinet will be torn down. So, I guess it's too late."

"No. Let's keep it in there, but update it. Let's just put a straight cash value on it for anyone, including the construction guys, if they find it. We can put our current addresses now," Tasha pleaded, and the other two went along with the new idea.

Once back in 407, they were joined briefly by President Riley who brought along a young Telecommunication major named Sophia.

"Wow. I can't believe I'm actually talking to you three," shrilled Sophia, "I mean the three of you are legends around here."

"So, who's your advisor?" asked Dawn in an attempt to put an end to the legend discussion.

"Professor Windsor, whom you don't know. He's only been here for about five years. And of course, Roger Gala, you know how he's helping us with our recruiting films. He's so talented. I've learned so much from him."

"I bet," Tasha snarled.

"So, as I understand it, Mr. Gala will be around this week?" Elizabeth said.

"Oh, I'm sure he wouldn't mind if you called him Roger. We all do. And yes, he'll be around, but he has a tendency to come and go."

"Literally, I'm sure," Tasha cracked, which caused Elizabeth and Dawn to give her that stare, the one stating that she ought to behave.

"And your schedules, ladies."

Tasha saw a great opportunity and went for it, "I will be here all week, but tomorrow night I have a location shoot. For some stupid tampon commercial. Not sure how late I will be."

"And on Wednesday, I'll be spending my token evening with my parents," Elizabeth added.

"And on Thursday, I have that Teen Hotline training. I'll probably be out quite late," Dawn offered.

Tasha was a bit disappointed. Roger had selected Tuesday evening because of his work schedule and Tasha was hoping that it would be the same night that the other two would be out. Oh well.

The rest of the day was not scheduled so the ladies had fun just roaming the campus and visiting former professors.

Then next morning, after a breakfast meeting with the president and various board members, the three went to the new, state of art filming center for their interviews, where they were interviewed individually and as a group.

They were just finishing up when they noticed all the young ladies in the room getting excited and rushing to the door. Behind, the mob, they could barely see one Roger Gala trying to step in.

After a few minutes of hugs and reassurances that they were lovely, Roger managed to work his way to the back room.

"So," he said, "how does it feel to be back on Mt. Olympus? I take it the little nymphs and centurions have been taking good care of you."

"Well, the centurions could be more groveling," Tasha responded.

"That's my fault. I instructed them not to. I told them they would get more of you if they played hard to get." Roger then leaned over and whispered in her ear, but loud enough so the other two could hear, "But really, they are craving for a little pat on the head from you, or even better, a pat on the butt." That breaking the ice, Roger then invited them for a cup of coffee over at the coffee shop.

"So, seriously, how are the future DGA members doing?" he asked as he placed the tray of drinks down on the table.

"They're doing fine. Very professional, I must say," Tasha answered.

"Great, I'm glad to hear that."

"The questions were excellent. Did you help write them?" Elizabeth asked.

"Oh yes," he said as he winked at her. "Well, I know I'll be seeing you three around. One of my flunkies will let you know when that will be. Until then, be kind to all the mere mortals," kissing each goddess's hand.

"Come back, Shane, come back," Tasha purred as the other two laughed.

Chapter twenty-one:
Aromatherapy 101

Tasha thanked the gods when all the little nymphs and centurions begged Elizabeth and Dawn to go to dinner with them. It gave Tasha a chance to be alone as she prepared for her evening with Roger. Exposed to her mystical wench look, her power suit, and even the relaxed look, it seemed Roger was more appreciative of the mystical wench, so Tasha decided upon a long wrap-around skirt, and a low-cut top that barely reached the skirt around her waist. Any movement of the arms would reveal her tight abs and navel, and hopefully put dirty thought into Roger's beautiful head.

Driving over to his Topanga house, she left the window open, to achieve an even more wind blown look, and she constantly checked the rear-view mirror to assure herself that her black eyeliner and burgundy lip stick were still perfect.

Turning off an old road, onto an even older road, she clicked on her brights, in an attempt to find any signs of life. Eventually, way down the road, she spotted what had to be his house—an old woodsy, two-story home with a front porch, thousands of wind chimes, stain glass hangings in the windows, out-of-control wildflowers, and a garage off to the side that appeared to house at least one car and one motorcycle.

As Tasha stepped out of the car, a gush of wind chilled her so she wrapped her shawl around her shoulders. A sweater would have been more effective against the cold, but would have impaired her grand entrance, and Tasha was a master at entrances.

Approaching the house, she could see the door slightly ajar almost inviting her in. She could hear tranquilizing new-age music, and smell the sensuous fragrances of almond, jasmine, lavender, and even a little sandalwood.

She entered the house and followed the music and scent to a room in the back. Inside the dimly lit room sat Roger, wearing only a pair of gauze, off-white drawstring pants, sitting in the classic yoga lotus position. Appreciating the serenity of meditation, she stepped out quietly and perused the various pictures and artifacts on his hallway wall.

"I didn't realize it was so late." His voice startled the hell out of her.

"I may be early."

"Oh, I doubt that. Not quite your style." He walked over and removed the shawl, stroking her arms on the way down. He then brought up his hands to her face, and used the back of his hands to brush back her hair.

"I'm sorry if I disturbed you."

"Are you kidding? Your spells are too strong to ignore."

He walked back into the room and returned buttoning a gauze shirt. As he passed Tasha, she reached out and unbuttoned what he had just buttoned.

"Well, you do deserve that reputation, don't you?"

"Don't be so cocky, I'm here to return the favor, on the massage table."

"Oh, that's right."

He approached, and Tasha fought back the urge to back up. Yes, he had gotten to her, but damn if she was going to show it.

"But first, may I ask one quick favor?

"Sure."

"May I film you? Here? The way you should be filmed?"

"I don't understand."

"All the cute campus chatter, joking around with roommates and young students, all so wholesome and full of family values. That's sufficient for Elizabeth and Dawn. But I'm an artist, and you're a muse. I say let's create some art."

"Direct me," she ordered.

He then took her hand and led her to another room that functioned as his studio.

Lights, camera and a sound system were all set and ready to go. He placed her standing in the center with a black backdrop behind her. He adjusted the lights so that they spotlighted on her.

Roger picked up the camera, and began walking around her. "Just getting my focus and feel." Tasha began to feel jittery and brought her hands up to play with her hair. "Do you want me seated?"

"Of course not. I'll just move the camera up when I need to," he said as he approached her and then circled her slowly. She smiled coyly for her close-up and with her head only, she followed the camera. Her years of ballet and yoga allowed her to stay with the camera longer than most mortal women, and when she reached as far as was humanly possible, she snapped her head and met up with the camera on the other side, only losing eye contact for a mere fraction of a second. Without words, there was a mutual agreement to continue this mating dance.

Roger finally turned off the camera and lowered it. For the next few moments, Tasha wondered if she had indeed learned anything over the years about letting masseurs become lovers.

When Roger finally walked away, she figured some matrimony goddess must have been looking out for her, but when she felt his hands brushing her hair back, she rationalized that she had been faithful for the most part during the last decade.

She could feel his lips and mustache on her neck as his left hand continued to weave in and out of hair. His right hand toyed with the bottom of her blouse. He gently pushed his tongue through his lips and began to make small circles around the front of her neck, and then gracefully moving to her side, and then her back.

"You know what I'm going to do?" he whispered.

"No."

"I'm going to lay you on your belly and put some almond oil all over your back. Then, I'm going to kiss every square inch of your back. And if I find a spot that makes you quiver when I kiss it—I'm going to kiss it again." He then bent down and lifted her over his shoulder and carried her upstairs to his bedroom where he indeed did what he had promised.

Once he completed that task, he turned her half-naked body over and placed her arms above her head. His pants were then removed and used as wrist restraints, securing her to the bedpost. With his teeth, he loosened the skirt, and with incredible agility and skill removed the remainder of her clothing without the help of any hands.

He poured almond oil into his palms, and began massaging her body, starting at one wrist, going down to the shoulder, then the other arm and wrist, and back down again. He caressed her breasts, glided his lips all over them, and then repeated the procedure on her belly and her hips. He lifted his head up and rubbed more oil into hands before rubbing her vagina and nearly making her insides explode with his tongue.

Tasha had been moaning all along, but the oral sex shifted her into overdrive, and she wrapped her legs around his neck, crossing her ankles. He, in turn, lifted her hips a few inches off the bed, so that her pelvic region was moving upwards as he smoothly thrusted in tongue down.

Tasha's moans became louder and louder and eventually turned into howls resembling something like a banshee. When she finally broke the decibel scale, he released himself and dropped her hips.

Laughing, he leaned over her to be face to face with her. "I'm only going to make you howl like that, let's see, maybe 20 or 30 times tonight." And he began again. It may not have been 20 or 30 times, but it was enough to make them both think that Tasha should audition for the next Werewolf movie.

At some point, Roger moved his hands up and untied the pants and gently helped Tasha sit up. They stared at each for a few seconds, and then Tasha, weak as she was, stood up and took his pants and wrapped them around her shoulders. She twirled and danced across his floor, performing every favorite move she could remember from all her jazz and belly dancing classes. A master of nonverbal communication she indicated with her hip movement, that he should lay down on his back and she moved in closer. She took his hands raised them over his head and stroked the gauze pants up and down his body, before securing his hands to the bed post. She then straddled him and dropped, from as high she could, cold little drops of almond on all over his body. She then bent over, and with her hair, massaged the oil into his soft skin.

This was followed by her creating the same lip action all over his chest, belly, and down to his groin, teasing every morsel of him, making him moan for completion, but she would then break away. The she would laugh and start again, until he again he moaned and she would break away.

"You little brat, just wait until I get free," he threatened.

Her teasing continued and finally, when she least expected it, he broke free, and sat up and threw her down on her back.

"I'm excited as hell, as you are. But, as you said, there is something to gaining wisdom." He then got off the bed. Tasha felt a rush of disappointment, but to her pleasant surprise, he opened a drawer and pulled out and put on a condom.

"I've never been with such a trained dancer before," he said, approaching her.

"And?"

"And this." He laid her on her back, grabbed onto her ankles and brought her knees up almost to her neck. He used him thumbs to massage her ankles, then he knelt down close to her, with his knees on either side of her and entered her from above. As his thumbs and fingers moved all over her feet, and her hands massaged his knees and thighs, they rocked together until they both felt a wonderful sense of blood rushing, and heart palpitating.

Exhausted, he fell down in need of breath. Tasha, although hyperventilating, was now full of new sexual energy. To accommodate both needs, he laid still on the bed as she massaged his feet.

When he began to rub her feet also, she knew he was catching his second wind.

And when he pulled out a joint and lit it, she knew the night was still young.

"Can you dance for me again?" he asked as they finished the joint.

"Yes."

Roger put on new music and Tasha twirled and gyrated around the floor, using as many erotic moves as possible. After a few rotations, Roger then caught up with her, spinning with her, his arms tightly around her waist. Then he lifted her and she crossed her ankles at the small of his back.

She was surprised to find him already erect and prepared. As he entered her and began to pump, she released her grip on his neck and fell backwards until she was completely upside down. Roger, who was not expecting that, caught her with his hands around her waist and continued to pump and moan.

As they were both climaxing, Tasha worried a bit that he might let go and drop her on her head. How the hell would she explain that bump? But, when finished, he pulled her up and with her legs still wrapped around him, began spinning extremely fast around the room, simulating one of the wild rides at an amusement park.

Crashing on his bed, they both remained still, unable to speak, but mustered up enough energy to stroke each other's hair and smoke another joint. "You're so beautiful," he said with what little energy he had left. "I love looking at you at this moment. You're just the picture of total serenity with an occasional burst of panic."

They continued stroking each other into the early hours, when Tasha finally announced she had better get back to the dorm.

"Can't believe I'm still saying that," she laughed.

"Don't go."

"I don't think it would be good idea for me to stay the night."

"And it would be a bad idea for you to leave now. You remember how treacherous those roads are at night. Besides, it's 3:00 a.m. You would have to come up with one hell of an explanation," he said as he got up and crossed over to his entertainment unit.

"I'll have to come up with one anyway," she reminded him.

"So you might as well stay," he pulled out a CD and inserted it into the player.

Tasha was about to respond when she heard the voices of Simon and Garfunkle singing *Wednesday Morning, 3 A.M.*

"You know they used those lyrics again," Tasha said.

"I know. *Somewhere They Can't Find Me. Sounds of Silence* album.

"Why are you playing it?" she asked suspiciously.

"Because it is now Wednesday morning. And it's 3 a.m. And I'm tired.

He rolled back the covers and guided Tasha underneath. As he held her tight, she mouthed the words, *My life seems unreal. My crime an illusion.* She began to feel there had to be some conspiracy going on. Or at least, something more than just a simple coincidence. But she could not articulate the allegations, much less prove them, so she decided to ignore it all and moved down deeper in Roger's bed and wrapped her arms across his chest.

It was about 5 in the morning when she next opened her eyes. Slowly moving, so not to disturb Roger, she stepped over him.

As she was picking up some of her clothing she felt his fingers stroking her arm.

"Don't go," he said as he began to kiss her arm.

"Oh, God. The spirit is willing, but the flesh is weak I'm afraid."

"Then let me do all the work"

Roger reached out and pulled her back in the bed. Laying her on her back he massaged her whole front body, first slowly, and then a little more vigorously. By the time he probed his fingers in between her thighs, she was already wet and he already had a new condom.

He spread her legs opened wider and turned over so that his legs were on either side of her with his feet at her face. Tasha instinctively rested her feet on his upper back and stroked his rear end as he penetrated her.

"Oh, shit," she moaned when they were through. "And I thought I was experienced."

"You're very inspirational."

"Thank you," she purred as he kissed her lips.

"This time, I really do have to be going," Tasha said with some regret.

"How about some breakfast? I owe you that."

"No you don't."

"Then how about I just want to. There is this wonderful bakery off of Old Topping Canyon Road. It has been there forever. And so has some of the bread. But it's great for a morning after?"

"And just how many women have you taken there for a morning after?"

"Just the special ones."

"Doesn't the waitress or baker or somebody tell your wife?"

"We're all aging hippies here. We take great pride in our unconventionality. Nobody wants to ruin it for anyone else. Last thing we want is to turn this Shangri-La into Peyton Place."

"How are the blueberry muffins?"

"Huge."

"Figures."

The morning air was cool and crisp so Roger handed her a sweatshirt to wear over her clothing. Once inside the bakery, Tasha looked around, and sure enough, everyone there had the freshly-fucked look about them.

"So what are you going to tell your roommates?" Roger finally asked.

"Something about the lighting and then how a bunch of young actors were adoring me and treated me to breakfast. You know, the usual crap."

"That's good. And no doubt, you'll pull if off," he said with admiration.

When they finished eating, Tasha drove him back to his house, and of course, returned the sweatshirt. As he walked toward his front door, he turned one last time and just stared. As she watched him become smaller and smaller in her rearview mirror, she sighed, "Fade out."

Wiping her nose, she felt a rush that only good dope could produce. "Oh shit," she laughed as she noticed the black spots on her acrylic nails. "I guess it's true. You play around, you get burned. Better make a nail appointment today," she laughed.

She took a deep breath before quietly entering 407 and was quickly relieved to find Elizabeth and Dawn fast asleep. As she began disrobing, she heard one of them, Elizabeth she believed, giggling and then it didn't matter, because both of them were laughing hysterically.

"Well, did you two really expect me to spend every night here?" she joked.

"Tradition," chimed in Dawn.

"Seriously, I was a little worried that Jacob would call and then it would be that whole George Weybourne thing again," said Elizabeth.

"George. What a sweetheart," Tasha said trying to change the subject. "I hope he attends the reunion this time. Do you know if he is, Elizabeth?"

"Shit, it's too early in the morning to think about that. I'm tempted to say no, but I can't be sure in this half-waken state of mind."

"Oh, God, ladies, it is going to be tough facing Jacob this weekend."

The two of them looked at her as if their worst thoughts had been realized.

"My cute little co-star in that stupid commercial talked me into an audition for one of his episodes."

"Oh mercy, not another stray cat," laughed Elizabeth.

"He's going to kill me."

"That's our girl," teased Dawn.

"So ladies, if you excuse me, I'm going to take a shower, then a nap."

As Tasha got into the shower, she examined her body closely and sure enough, just as she expected, a hickey on the inside of her thigh and another one down on her hip bone.

"That bastard," she laughed as she turned on the hot water. She then leaned against the shower wall and sighed gently with a smile on her face. "That bastard."

Chapter twenty-two:

Dawn 101

As Tasha climbed into bed for her morning nap, those who were not so sleep-deprived prepared for their day of interviews, Phi Beta Kappa meetings, class visitations, and lunch with the faculty senate.

"I see Tasha is still sleeping in after a fun night," commented a Political Science professor who had the misfortune of having Tasha enrolled in one of his morning classes nearly twenty-three ago.   Dawn and Elizabeth just smiled and nodded.

Tasha did wake up in time for her nail appointment, and somehow managed to arrive on time to view, judge, and present awards at the Annual Student-Directed One-Act Play Festival. And, of course, being one of the more successful graduates of the Theatre Arts Department, she felt an obligation to attend the reception that evening at the house of the Dean of Fine Arts—with Dawn as her escort, thanks to the persuasion skills of one Marin County attorney.

"Thanks for coming with me," Tasha said as they entered Tudor Hall, 407.

"No, thank you. To tell you the truth, with Elizabeth at her parents tonight, I would have been afraid to be here all alone," Dawn said as she sat on a bed.

"Really?" Tasha said as she snuggled up next to her on the bed. "I guess I never really picture you afraid." Dawn just looked at her. "But you are now, at work, huh?"

"Tasha, I just don't know what I'm going to do. I love many aspects of my job. It's just that we are so poorly managed and so under funded, that we've become ineffective. I'm almost embarrassed to take on new clients.

I'm thinking about resigning and I don't know, going into computers or something."

"That would be a waste," Tasha said. "And I have to agree with Elizabeth. Why don't you apply to be the director?"

"I know you two have this image of me being so in control and organized. And in a sense, I am. But there's more to the job than just overseeing the center."

"Like what?"

"Fundraising. Public Relations. Lots and lots of dinners and handshaking and you know that's something for you, not me."

"I disagree but I'm not going to argue that point now, because I think there's some unknown elements involve. My instincts tell me that when you say you are considering a career change, you are actually running away from something as oppose to running to something."

Dawn just turned and looked at her, "Who are you and where's my free-spirited roomie, Tasha?"

Tasha laughed, "I know, I have no idea where that bit of insight came from. Must be some old line from one of my old movies."

Dawn laughed, too. "Well, keep going with the script, because I think you're on to something."

"What?" Tasha asked softly.

Dawn laid her head on Tasha's shoulder. "Miranda never forgave me for siding against her when we both served on the Rape Awareness Symposium Committee. And even though the project was a huge success and she received a lot of public credit, she still threw it in my face that we had actually let the victims on our campus down. I always ignored her, but one evening, about a week before she disappeared, we got into another argument. I was tired and told her she needed help with her anger problem. And then..."

"What, Dawn?"

"Miranda looked at me severely, and told me that since I was the product of a gang rape, that I was incapable of thinking badly of the rapists, you know, my father-fantasy figure or something. She also said that since my mother had managed to return to school and become a librarian, that I had no concept how a life could be ruined by a rape. She said she regretted ever getting me on the committee."

Tasha moved in close to Dawn and brushed away some of the tears. "You know, she was quite brutal at times. I'm sorry you had to hear that, Dawn."

"But the sad thing was, that was practically the last thing she ever said to me. A week later, Kip was dead, and Miranda was gone."

"Oh my god, I didn't know."

"And you know, what is so pathetic, I think I looked for evidence that she killed Kip. I truly wanted to believe that she was capable of killing someone, because it would discredit all her accusations, and what she had said to me. I could go on thinking she was just a neurotic extremist."

"In many ways, she was, Dawn."

"But now, with all these new revelations, my god, she was right. There were young women who were harmed on campus, and we did nothing for them."

"It wasn't your job, Dawn. And the symposium did a lot of good. There were numerous guests. A lot of good panels and information regarding self-defense and prevention."

"Apparently it didn't stop the crimes."

"Listen, Dawn, after this week, I'm going to present all the stuff you have given me to Roger. I've already spoken to him, and he's going to pursue the subject and make a documentary."

"I don't know what that will accomplish."

"I know I'm not the right person to be saying this, but for the time being, can you trust me?"

Dawn looked at her and they both broke out laughing. "Sure, what's there to lose?"

Tasha held Dawn tightly and stroked her long hair, giving her a chance to finally enjoy a good cry. Eventually they fell into a beautiful deep sleep, only to be awakened at the crack of dawn by Elizabeth's entrance.

"Why's the roommate always the last to know," Elizabeth said noticing the two of them in one bed.

"Good morning. And I do mean, morning" Tasha yawned. "So, how was the reunion?"

"God, my mother can find more topics to bitch about, and of course, my father had to go over all the family finances. Plus, he still has this fantasy that I'm going to quit the practice and become his in house attorney, and maybe even his heir apparent."

"Sounds like a grand evening," Tasha teased.

"Oh, it was. And now if you excuse me, I need to take a shower."

Chapter twenty-three:
Elizabeth 101

Later that early evening, as the three primped for the cocktail party the Faculty Club was sponsoring for some generous patrons, Elizabeth gave them the word about proper decorum.

"Don't fret, Elizabeth, I've slummed it before," teased Tasha, as she lined her lips with Harley Red.

"Please, I helped put this shindig together, so just behave, both of you," Elizabeth lectured.

"Excuse me, Elizabeth?" Dawn questioned, stopping her hairbrush in midstroke.

"Sorry," Elizabeth put down her make-up bag. "Behave yourself, Tasha."

"I who attend the Emmys, the Tonys."

"I never said you didn't know how to behave. What I am strongly implying is that you sometimes choose not to behave."

"Philistine."

"Especially, if you know that the situation is conducive to shock value," Elizabeth continued.

"Okay! Okay! I will make nice with them. I will pretend to have some interest in their pitiful, pathetic lives."

"Thank you, Tasha."

"You know, but some girls have all the luck. If I had remembered that you had coerced us into attending this affair tonight, I would have signed up for Dawn's hotline training session."

"Oh no, you cannot hog your way into this. This is my deal. And only my deal," Dawn said defending her turf.

"That reminds me," Elizabeth reopened her bag and pulled out a compact, "I was talking to Ed."

"Who's Ed?" Tasha inquired.

"President Riley."

"Ed? You call him Ed?"

"Yes. That is his name. Anyway, I was talking to him earlier today."

"And yesterday, and the day before that."

Dawn giggled at their volley.

"Well, I am the honored guest this week."

"It just seems you guys are in contact quite a bit."

"Not really."

"I mean, how..."

"Tasha!" Elizabeth screamed before regaining her composure. "You know, if you ever get a divorce, I just might represent Jacob."

"Okay, continue."

"Thank you. As I was saying, when I spoke to Ed, AKA, President Riley, I made arrangements for him to drive you and me home, Tasha, and don't even go there. That way, Dawn can take the car and leave early for her appointment."

"She gets to leave early?"

Dawn giggled again.

"Yes, Tasha, she does."

"Some girls have all the luck."

At hotel conference room, the three made a stunning entrance, with Elizabeth in a short black beaded dress with long sleeves, Tasha in a red halter gown, and Dawn in a long white slip dress.

"Good evening, ladies," Ed Riley addressed them. "Elizabeth, I don't believe you have had a chance to meet our newest board member, Edmund Beck, CEO of WSS Investments.

Edmund Beck, a short bald man, shook hands with both Elizabeth and Tasha, but kept a hold of Dawn's as he pulled her to the side and began telling his saga of traveling to the Grand Canyon and what a mystical journey it had been; so mystical, the he even purchased a Navajo rug, now hanging in his office, not to mention a few Kachina Dolls.

"Do you think we should rescue her?" Tasha whispered to Elizabeth.

"Wait a few minutes. He's responsible for some major high tech donations coming in."

"You mean to tell me, you would sell out Dawn for some big donations?"

"Oh yeah. I've sold you for some puny ones. Oh there's Marc, I need to talk to him," Elizabeth said before bolting off.

"Shit," Tasha said nearly spilling her drink as she felt a pair of hands grab her around the waist.

"Tasha, so nice to see you again. It's been way too long," Tasha immediately recognized John Morgan's voice and turned to give him a big hug. Who said she wasn't a good actress.

"So how's my favorite actress?" he asked still holding onto her.

"Just fine. And how's my favorite, oh what the hell were you anyway?" she teased.

John placed his face to hers and whispered, "I don't know, but whatever it was, I'm willing, ready, and able to be it again."

"You are still ever so charming."

"And available all next week. Why don't you come by?"

Tasha fought her natural urge to stiffen up. "I'll check my schedule and see what I have open," she said stalling him.

"You know, dear, I haven't seen you in too many things lately. You're not working like you should. And I still have my influences." Tasha didn't like the sound of that, but she played dumb very well.

"I bet you do. I'll call you on Monday." John then grabbed a quick kiss and wandered off.

"Wow, does Jacob know about him?" Elizabeth said behind her.

"Jesus Christ, I wish people would quit sneaking up on me," Tasha said as she jumped back a bit, barely missing her dress with her flying drink.

"Well don't you two look heavenly," a voice from behind them came.

The two quickly turned to find themselves facing a rather dashing Roger Gala, attired in classic tuxedo and combed hair no less.

Tasha was the first to speak, "Well, as Carly Simon phrased it, 'You're where you should be all the time and when you're not.'"

"Oh, we won't go there now, will we ladies?" he said as he first kissed Elizabeth's hand and then Tasha's. "Ah, and lovely nails this evening," he said as he winked at Tasha.

"So are you one of the important and distinguished alumni or big time contributors Elizabeth was warning me about?" Tasha smiled.

"Hardly. I'm just one of those overdressed video recorders, recording your triumphant return to campus."

About this time, Dawn, who was already bored and moving toward insulted by Edmund's benign and unenlightened discourse on Indian Arts and Crafts, walked graciously away and up to her roommates.

"And you look lovely, also, Miss Wolfe," Roger said. "Now if you three don't mind, please mingle with all these community bigwigs, so I can show potential students how they too can come to PCU and end up exchanging amusing discourse with some of the most influential leaders of today."

"You actually believe any of that shit you just said?" Tasha asked.

"Hell, no. But honey, remember the poor starving artist. Hunger creates more whores than anything."

After working the room, the three somehow ended up in the corner, laughing and making faces into the camera."

"Okay, okay, I think we have enough footage," Roger said, knowing it would be futile to push the goddesses any more.

"Good, because I'm going to have to leave in a few minutes," Dawn reminded them.

"Oh yeah, your stint at the Teen Center or something. Well, you will truly be voted the best dressed counselor," Roger said.

"Actually, I'm stopping back at the campus to change. And then one of the directors is picking me up. Maybe I should take your keys now, Tasha?"

"I can give you lift. I have to leave in a few minutes myself," Roger said.

"Oh, please," Elizabeth lectured, "she is not exactly dressed for your Harley."

"No Harley this evening. I've got a limo. Ready, Dawn?" he walked between Elizabeth and Tasha, and offering his arm to Dawn.

"I guess," she responded somewhat flustered, but pleasantly surprised, before taking his arm.

"Did we just cancel each other out?" Tasha asked.

Elizabeth soothed Tahsa's bruised ego by finding a group of men to worship her, while Tasha focused on the fact that Roger always seemed to chauffeuring Dawn around in some exclusive vehicle.

Later that evening, back in the dorm, Tasha watched Elizabeth arrange and rearrange the items on her dresser.

"Something wrong, goddess of the reunion?"

"I just couldn't help noticing how much you flirted with John Morgan," Elizabeth finally admitted.

"Well, I couldn't help noticing how much you discussed some business contracts with him," Tasha shot back, almost hating herself immediately for doing so.

"Touché! But, what can I do? He and my father recently bought a huge interest in a company, and I negotiated everything for them. And well, I don't want John to suspect that I now know what I know. So, I guess I was trying to act normal."

"And I don't want John to suspect that I know what I know, so I, too, was trying to act normal." Tasha noticed the look of disapproval on Elizabeth's face. "It's just that normal for me isn't normal for you."

"Oh Tasha, normal for you isn't normal for anyone else on this planet," Elizabeth said allowing a slight smile to emerge. "John is one of the biggest womanizers. He remains on the Board of Trustees for no other reason than to have an excuse to hang around a bunch of eighteen-year-olds, and who does he turn to mush for? You. Twenty years out of college."

"And you're surprised because?"

"I'm not surprised. Just stating a fact," Elizabeth said with true admiration. "But enough of stroking your ego. Speaking of knowing what we know. What are we going to do with this newfound knowledge?"

Tasha crawled onto Elizabeth's bed and sat close to her. "I think we should have Roger make a documentary. We can turn everything over to him as anonymous sources and boom, John Morgan and his merry men will never see it coming."

Elizabeth leaned into Tasha more. "And neither will my father or Ed. But then, maybe that would be for the best, I don't know."

"Who's Ed?"

"Riley, you moron," Elizabeth laughed. "The current PCU president."

"Oh, yes, your adoring male."

"Oh, please, we're just..."

"If you say friends, I'm going to bop you one. This is me Tasha, remember? I can smell sexual tension a mile away."

Elizabeth blushed a little. "Well, yes, there is that unspoken mutual admiration thing going on. But," she quickly emphasized, "that's all. There has never been any inappropriate behavior between us."

"Why not?" Tasha sincerely asked.

"Tasha!" Elizabeth screeched. "I swear you are the only person who would ask that question. Believe it or not, some of us enjoy fidelity."

Tasha couldn't help but to enjoy Elizabeth's squirming at the moment.

"So you don't think you would ever..."

"Tasha, Ed is quite a distinguished, intelligent, charming man. I have one of those at home. If I were ever to break my vows, I would go for something totally different."

"Like Roger?"

"What?" she screeched again only louder.

"Well, you once had an affinity for motorcycle guys, and he took you to a bar."

Maybe it was the wine, but Elizabeth snuggled down and placed her head on Tasha's shoulder.

"You know, goddess, you are the only person I can confess this to. I had a blast on that bike and in that bar. It's not a place I want to live full-time, but it would be fun to visit occasionally."

"Then why don't you?"

"Tasha, please, I have my family, my career, my reputation."

"Your hang-ups, your fears."

"I don't deny all that. And maybe that's good. Maybe that's what's keeping me from jumping on your mid-life journey," she sighed. "Listen, all this Miranda stuff, and maybe Roger's documentary are enough excitement for me to handle. I'm going to keep letting you be the wild one."

"Say, Johnny what are you rebelling against?"

"What you got?" they said in unison, laughing before stretching out and falling asleep in each other's arms.

"Well, I always knew you hated sleeping alone, Tasha, but..." Dawn said bright and early the next morning as she entered the room.

"My god, are you just getting in?" Elizabeth asked groggily?

"Yes. It was quite an eventful evening. We had a suicidal person on the phone."

"Oh. my god, is everything okay?" Tasha asked.

"Yes. She is under care now. And I think she will be okay. But the poor trainees. Wow, they got a good taste of what's involved." Just then there was a knock on the door.

"What the hell," sniped Tasha.

"Hello, it's me, Sophia."

Since Dawn was the one standing there, she was the one who let her in.

"Good morning, ladies," Sophia said with way too much energy. "I'm sorry about this early hour, but I wanted to catch you early."

"Mission accomplished," Tasha said in an unfriendly tone.

"I just wanted to go over the schedule for today. And of course, we won't be bugging you this evening."

"Why?" they chorused.

"Well, it's been five days. I mean, isn't today when your husbands arrive?"

"Oh yeah," they all muttered.

Chapter twenty-four:

Saturday's Child

It wasn't that Tasha wasn't happy to see Jacob or to actually spend the night in a beautiful hotel suite; it was just that she had recently been unfaithful and was somewhat worried that she would give off a scent or make some stupid faux pas, cluing her husband in. His presence also created some anxiety in her in that he represented the coming of the reunion weekend, which would be followed by the end of the reunion weekend, which would be followed by her keeping the promise that she would finally get Miranda exonerated. And while the end result was honorable, it was the means that upset her. But in her hedonistic fashion, she decided that the impending doom and fallout didn't have to interfere with all the festivities, especially the ones in which she would be the center of attention.

After Friday, when the three goddesses and their spouses closed down the hotel bar, Saturday afternoon was devoted to the game. While Elizabeth totally outshone all the other past queens on their floats, Tasha hogged the spotlight in the stands, flitting about and signing autographs.

But Saturday evening was the big event. Totally aware that they were escorting goddesses, the three husbands rose to the occasion and donned tuxedos. They also were smart enough to stand back and allowed the three to make their grand entrances, filmed by Roger.

Dawn provided an elegant picture in a full-length bronze lame halter dress, with a slit up the side. Her hair glimmered to the maximum, shining brightly, and hanging straight. Elizabeth looked stunning in a long black glittering dress with long sleeves, high neck in the front, but a plunging drop in the back. Her blonde bob had been styled to give it more height and glamour. And the actress entered the hall in a silvery shimmering godet gown, with a swirl around her ankles, accentuating her full breasts, and the rest of her hour glass physique. Her feet were strapped in five inch silver stilettos sandals and her hair was in a classic French roll with a few curls hanging by the face.

"So, should I be careful and not record what half the guys say to you," teased Roger, snuggling up to her.

"Oh, my dear, Jacob knew what he was getting when he married me. But I bet most of the wives here would shit if they knew I provided their husbands with the best sex they ever had. So, you might want to put on the mute button."

"A little sure of yourself," he said.

"Honey, look at them. Every one of them lusting after me still," and then she stopped short and began to stare off into the distant.

"What?" Roger asked as he looked around, trying to figure out what the hell could draw attention from herself.

"That son of a bitch."

"Yeah, I better put on the mute button. What?" he said still examining the room, totally confused.

"George Weybourne. One of my guys. Why the fuck is he there in the corner talking with Dawn?"

"Maybe he liked her, too," Roger said indicating he could not believe her attitude.

"He hardly knew her. Dawn didn't have the collection of men that Elizabeth and I had. And Elizabeth didn't have quite as many as I did." She started walking, but Roger actually pulled on her dress to bring her back.

"Whoa, goddess. Image, remember your image. Show some compassion for the less beautiful, okay."

Tasha swirled around in a fury and faced him head on. "Well aren't you Dawn's new best friend? Jaguar, limo, and now one of my guys. I suppose you'll give her the best lighting, too?"

She hated herself for lashing out, and hated herself even more for not understanding why she was feeling so insecure and threatened in the first place. Although, with Roger was standing before her with a total hard-on, fighting back the urge to just lay a big kiss on her was doing wonders for her self-esteem.

"You need some discipline, darling, and I intend to hand it out later. But you'll have to excuse me; it's almost time for me to pay some of attention to the guest of honor. You may know her, she's been described as the goddess of classic beauty and charm," he said just to push her buttons.

"Or the ice queen who jumped on the back of your Harley. Your call," she shot back.

"It's ironic that you don't approve of the rides I gave them, when I probably gave you the best ride of all a few nights ago. But it is fun to see you jealous for a change."

"I'm not jealous I'm just..." she stumbled for a word that just didn't come.

"Jealous," he said victoriously.

"Yeah," she said in defeat. "Haven't a clue as to why. It's just that, hell, I don't know. You know we goddesses got along so well, because we never treaded onto each other's turf."

"Didn't realize men were chattel."

"Don't be so ornery with me. I swear I don't know what is going on, I mean I have never been so competitive with my friends, until you popped into our lives..." she stopped short again and stared at him.

"What?" he asked one again confused.

"Well, aren't you a cute little apple?"

"Excuse me? Granted my last name is Gala, but..." he didn't finish the sentence but indicated with his hands that he was still confused.

"Who sent you? Who tossed you into our lives?"

"I don't know what you're talking about, I swear," he pleaded with total sincerity.

"You probably don't," she conceded shaking her head. "Listen, you sweet delicious thing. Go and film Elizabeth's big moment, and Dawn's triumphant return to campus, but there is only enough soft lighting for one goddess and that goes to me."

"Yes, ma'am."

Tasha watched him walk away in wonder, and then muttered softly to herself. "Fuck, it's either you Miranda, or those devious fates. Either way, I better enjoy tonight, because I feel a bad storm brewing."

Regardless of that ominous feeling, Tasha did manage to enjoy the rest of the evening, especially since it was she who commanded the largest audience with tales of Hollywood. She did, however, graciously allow Elizabeth to take center stage when the President Riley entered the room, sans his wife, Tasha noted, and presented Elizabeth with the *Walter Tudor Outstanding Alumnus Award* and announced that the new Student Government Building would be named after her, an honor which even surprised the recipient.

After the party officially ended in the hall, it worked it way up a few flights and landed in the suite of the goddesses until almost dawn.

After the last guest left, Tasha stood outside on the balcony and watched in amazement at the ambitious early morning joggers and dog walkers already up and about.

"Oh, shit," she yelled as Jacob's hands around her waist startled her.

"Wow, a little jumpy," he laughed, as he held her close. "Worried about how you are going to look later in the harsh daylight?" he teased.

"Sunglasses and a cute hat will cover a multitude of sins, you should know that by now," she bantered back. But he was right, she was jumpy, but not because of the impending picnic the next day. Tasha could have sworn that one of those nauseating health freaks out there running at that ungodly hour was none other than Miranda herself; but when Jacob interrupted her focus, she lost sight of the runner.

"Poor thing. You are shivering. Why don't we go and heat things up until the picnic?" he offered.

"And sleep?" she toyed with him.

"We can get it next week. You know, it would be fun to be loud for no other reason than to annoy the other couples," he laughed.

Tasha was game for more sex, this time actually with her husband; but strangely, no amount of amorous play cleared her mind of

that jogger or her gut feeling that Pandora
was soon going to open her box.

Chapter twenty-five:
Sunday, Bloody, Sunday

Tasha was about to let out another orgasmic howl, when there was loud banging on the main door. "Jesus, honey, there's banging going on all over the place," she said to Jacob who was too busy ejaculating to give a damn about her little double entendre.

"Elizabeth! Thank god you're up" Tasha could hear President Riley say frantically as he entered their suite.

"Jesus, I knew he was infatuated, but not this obsessed," she said throwing a much chagrined Jacob off her so she could get up and listen by the door.

"Ouch! Fuck it, can't you knock?" hollered Tasha as she was clobbered by the door when Elizabeth burst in.

"Shit, it was no secret what you two are up to. And I don't give a damn that you're naked," Elizabeth said as she grabbed Tasha's arm and dragged her through the living room area, over to Dawn, who standing in front of her door.

"My god, what is it?" Dawn asked fastening her robe.

"My room! Now!" Elizabeth commanded. She then dragged the two of them into her room, barked orders for her husband to leave and excitedly picked up the front page of the Sunday morning paper. She began reading aloud an article about the death of Kip Morgan and the conspiracy to frame Miranda Taylor for his murder.

In a well-researched, well-documented, not to mention, well-written piece, reporter Tonya Giordi, a recent PCU grad, presented an accurate portrayal of that evening's events, and the manipulations and payoffs that

265

followed. Many of the allegations made in the article were supported by quotes from many of the principal characters in the saga including Jack Scwhartz of the Topanga Sheriff's Department; George Weybourne, a classmate of Kip's as well as admitted rapist; and Karen Dobson and Stephanie Borghese, two of the victims. The article also provided readers with pictures of the spoils of war panties and the check made out to Mr. Borghese. Tasha sat there wrapped only in blanket, shaking, distraught by the idea that her beloved George Weybourne was involved.

"Tasha. Is it just me, or does some of the evidence presented here look familiar?" Elizabeth asked sarcastically.

"I don't want to add to the stress level," Dawn chimed in, "and I'm not accusing you of anything, Tasha, but I trusted you with those panties and that check. Plus how did you know it was George Weybourne with whom I spoke?"

"I didn't know it was George. At least until now. And I swear to you both, I don't know who this Tanya chick is or how she got her hands on anything."

"I should know better, but somehow I believe you," said Elizabeth still frustrated at not knowing what was going on.

"You know what is really strange?" Tasha asked, ignoring the look from her two friends that said they thought she was from another planet.

"Think about it. This article is full of a lot of evidence that only a few people were privy to."

"You mean us," Elizabeth reminded her.

"Yes," Tasha said agreeing with her. "But, with the exception of one brief paragraph, naming us as her totally baffled roommates, we are not mentioned at all."

"Can't believe you're upset about the lack of free publicity at this moment," Elizabeth said with quite a bit of judgment.

"I'm not," she growled. "In fact, I'm relieved. But I'm also intrigued. Don't the two of you get it? Someone out there has been using us, but also protecting us."

Dawn and Elizabeth looked at each, realizing that for once, Tasha made a valid deduction.

"Roger," they all said in unison.

"Okay, ladies, here's the plan," Elizabeth announced. "We will put our best faces forward today at the picnic. We will not answer any questions, not from reporters, not from classmates. And tonight, instead of going back to Tasha's house with husbands and children, we will spend the night at Tudor and figure out what to do with dear Roger."

Just then the door opened, and President Riley walked in. "I know I'm intruding, but now that you have read the story, I think you can see where I need your help. This is going to create such controversy and reopen so many old wounds. Listen, Elizabeth, some of your classmates are already up and are reading this as we speak. I need you to present a unifying speech; like you did 20 years ago and then go on out to the family picnic, and fuck it." He paced around the room. "Go have a good time. That should hold the reporters and the parents and everyone else at bay until I figure this whole thing out."

A little before 11:00 that morning, all six were escorted down to the lobby by President Riley, where reporters and many of their classmates waited.

Tasha and Dawn felt someone tap their shoulders and turned around to see George Weybourne.

"Well, Dawn, I guess you now know why I wanted to talk to you next week. And Tasha, God, I hope you don't hate me, but I wouldn't blame you if you did. But either way, please believe me when I tell you I had no idea this story was going to break today. The lady said it would be a few months at least."

"What lady?" Dawn asked.

"The reporter, Tonya Giordi."

"How did she know to call you? I promise you, George, I did not mention our conversation to anyone..."

"Oh, I know that, Dawn. You are the most genuine person I know and your word is good enough for me. I think it was Karen who gave her my name. To tell you the truth, considering the harm I have caused to some women on campus, I didn't think I was in the position to be worried about who was naming me. I figured God sent her to me so I could tell the story and hopefully help the victims in the healing process."

"You did a good thing, George," Dawn assured him with a hug.

"Thank you. And while I feel weird, knowing that my classmates are looking at me knowing what I did, I'm not afraid about what is going to happen. The Lord may not spare me any punishment or pain, but he is holding my hand tightly, and he will continue to do so. And my family's, too."

"I hope you don't regret attending this reunion," Dawn said.

"No, I don't I had a great time last night and let's face it, I have to face my past sometime." He took her hands and continued, "Last night, I realized I had so many wonderful memories and there were so many great people on campus. I just made the mistake of joining the wrong group my first year, for all the wrong reasons. I am also guilty of not speaking up when I should have." He straightened his shoulders. "Well I'm speaking up now." He then embraced both Dawn and Tasha while they listened to Elizabeth's statement.

"Fellow classmates, members of the press, and President Riley," Elizabeth began, "PCU has always stood for the search of the truth, no matter how long the journey, how tedious the task. Today, after nearly 20 years of unanswered questions, we are now presented with an abundance of new information regarding that dark episode of our college career: The tragic death of Kip Morgan and the allegations of Miranda Taylor committing murder."

She waited for the murmurs to lessen, and then continued.

"The new evidence presented today creates a new picture. One where Kip Morgan was merely a victim of a freak accident, and Miranda was a victim of her fear and mistrust of the legal system."

More murmurs, louder this time and Elizabeth had to her throat, to subtly regain the crowd's attention.

"We have found the truth. We must now continue the journey, seeking reasoning, forgiveness, and healing. I know most of us have always believed in Miranda's innocence. Miranda, while turbulent and confrontational, was a foe of violence. Physically harming another human being would only distract from what she held most sacred: The power of the pen. And it is most fitting that today, we now know the truth, due to the efforts and hard work of someone who followed in Miranda's footsteps. PCU Journalism graduate, Tonya Giordi."

"I could remain angry over how my friend's life has been ruined by all the lies and deception. But today, I would like to celebrate the innocence of Miranda Taylor and what might be the beginning of a closure. I would like to extend my arms out to Miranda and let her know that our prayers and good thoughts are still with her and that we all would like some assurance that she is safe. Please come home now, Miranda. The door is officially open."

Many classmates applauded at that point. Elizabeth looked around and then spoke, "Now, let's have that picnic, with our loved ones, and our old friends. I will see you at Topanga Park." A few reporters tried to ask questions, but Elizabeth announced that she was eager to see her children at the picnic, and they could reach her at her office during the week, if they had any more questions.

The picnic had a strange but exciting feel to it. On one level, everyone was walking on eggshells, but on another, there was a strong sense of camaraderie, as if they had all been through a crisis together and survived.

Rumors began to circulate that Miranda might even show. But by 5:00, and a few false Miranda sightings, it was evident that she wouldn't. People were starting to pack up, when Kevin Tennyson, a former DJ on the campus station and now a morning voice in Portland, put on his boom box the Steely Dan classic, *My Old School*. Then he played it again. By the third time, there were enough slightly intoxicated boomers who were willing to stand on top of the picnic tables and sing along, much to the chagrin of their children.

Then Kevin followed that with some timely classics and began to pass around microphone, allowing people to express their inner feelings at the moment. When the mike reached George, there seemed to be some tension for a few moments, but then he asked if people would mind if he said a prayer. One, to ask God for his forgiveness, and two, to ask for Miranda's safety and for her appearance at the 25th anniversary. On that request, everyone applauded, and without any formal instruction, people just formed a circle and held hands while he led them in prayer. When finished, Kevin put on the Youngbloods, *Get Together* and the alumni continued to hold hands, as they swayed and sang along. The next generation bonded in mass humiliations of their parents' antics.

Afterwards, George's wife, Cindy, approached Tasha and Dawn and thanked Dawn for calling her husband that fateful day. "God truly sent you."

"Well, I don't know if it was God..." Dawn admitted.

"It was. God appears differently to different people."

So that was it, Tasha thought. Roger Gala is God. What a horrifying thought.

Later as they were loading up the car, Tasha begged Elizabeth to reconsider her earlier order.

"Elizabeth, are you sure we can't discuss things in my hot tub as oppose to 407?" Tasha pleaded.

"No," she answered emphatically.

"But we have all the kids." Jacob brought up.

"Oh, hell, order pizza and pick up some video games. How hard can that be?" Elizabeth was in real bitch mode.

With that order given, the men and the children returned to Beverly Hills, without the right amount of seatbelts in the van. And the ladies took the BMW back to Tudor.

Chapter twenty-six:
Revelations

"What are these?" Elizabeth asked suspiciously of the three wrapped presents waiting for them in 407.

"Relax, Elizabeth. They're just appreciation gifts from the film students," Tasha said reading her note. "Hey look, this is practically the same red nightgown I wore the first night here. How cute." Tasha then turned around and saw that Elizabeth and Dawn also received a replica of their first evening's nightwear.

"This is sweet of them. But considering their guru, I think we need to remember that one should beware of Greeks bearing gifts," advised Elizabeth.

Tasha would have agreed, but she was intrigued by Dawn's complete focus on a note that came with her t-shirt, and the fact that Dawn was now pulling out her old yearbook.

"I say we call Roger up and set up a meeting, like now," Elizabeth continued. "Unless of course, he left town or something, the coward."

"Well, actually," Tasha recalled, "I think he said something about doing something with his wife today."

"You mean his ex-wife," Elizabeth corrected her.

"No, I mean his wife, Renee" Tasha was getting fed up with Elizabeth's addiction to always being right.

"Yes, Renee, the wife he divorced a few years ago."

"Well, actually he told me," Dawn jumped in, "that Renee was a girlfriend, and that he has never been married. But who's counting?"

"You mean we all were told a different story about his marital status. What else has he been bullshitting us with? This warrants a confrontation now. If we have to, I can get my P.I. on the case to track the fucker down," Elizabeth paced furiously back and forth in that room.

"Or we can just go to our bathroom," Dawn suggested.

"Now why would we do that?" Elizabeth scowled.

"Because he's there waiting for us. In fact, I believe he's been waiting for us to come to him for 20 years," Dawn answered.

"What do you mean?" Tasha asked somewhat spooked by the turn of events.

"Evidence number one. Our note from the bathroom with an added message which read: *No need to send a reward. We've all been rewarded. Thank you. Thank you. Thank you. Love Roger.* And then you notice the smaller message, *When did mediocrity become such a sin?*"

Tasha and Elizabeth grabbed each other's hand.

Dawn continued, "Evidence number two. Notice this picture yearbook, Olympia Hall, 1973. Elisha Roger Galah. Think about it. Take away those thick glasses. Erase the acne. Give him a decent haircut. Buff up the shoulders a little..."

"And change his name," Tasha interrupted. "What is going on?"

"Time to find out, ladies. Let's march," ordered Elizabeth as she marched out the door like a general followed by her two loyal lieutenants.

When they reached the bathroom, Elizabeth swung open the door to find one Roger Gala, complete in jeans, t-shirt and leather jacket, sitting on the tub, in Miranda's old spot, lighting up a joint.

"I knew you three would one day come to me," he joked.

"You know, if I hadn't seen that old yearbook picture, I would be wondering if this was Miranda, post-Stockholm," Tasha whispered, but not too softly.

"Except I don't know if a transsexual can ejaculate real sperm," Dawn blurted out before she could stop herself.

"What?" Tasha shrieked, realizing that her beloved Roger had been rather beloved with one of the other goddesses. Now the only question was, did she want to strangle Dawn first or Roger first?

"Well, well," Elizabeth said in her attorney's voice. "Dawn just did us a service by accidentally admitting to a physical relation with you. And I will now confess to such a relation with you..."

"What?" Tasha shrieked even louder. This time, there was no contest; Roger was to be the first victim.

"Tasha, quiet or you will be asked to leave," Elizabeth demanded.

"Excuse me," Tasha crossed her arms, "this is not your courtroom."

"Watch me," Elizabeth challenged as she physically escorted Tasha to her old place on the toilet. "Now you sit, be quiet, and let me do the interrogating." Then she turned and faced her other roommate. "Dawn," she snapped and Dawn obediently sat on the floor against the tub.

"Good," Elizabeth said examining her environment. "Okay, now Mr. Gala, or whatever your name is, it's been established that both Dawn and I have been fucked by you. And if we have been fucked by you, then it's a given that Tasha has been fucked by you."

Tasha just threw up her hands and figured it would be awhile before she received any respect in this trial.

"So now that it has been established that we've all been fucked. Would it be too much to ask why?"

"You three weren't fucked. You were seduced. Willingly and happily, I may add," the defendant responded.

"What?" Tasha couldn't help herself. She shrieked on a decibel level that caused the other three to her cover their ears.

"Shut up!" The three yelled in unison.

Elizabeth cleared her throat. "Let me rephrase the question, then. It has been established that we've all been seduced. Willing and happily you might add. Would it be too much to ask why?"

Roger looked around the bathroom, smiling slyly, "To fulfill both a fantasy and an obligation."

"To fuck the three goddesses of 407?" Elizabeth yelled.

"Four. There are four goddesses of 407," he reminded her.

"And you." Dawn started carefully.

"Fucked all four. Well, actually, I prefer the term, seduced, but how many men can make that claim?"

"Well, when we're through with you..." Tasha yelled as she got up, only to be pushed back down by Elizabeth.

"You've been warned," Elizabeth said looking down on her. "And you," she said to Roger. "The truth, from the beginning. The truth. The whole truth. And nothing but the truth. So help you the goddesses of 407." She then walked confidently over to the heater and resumed her seat of authority.

Roger took a hit. "I was always your classic Geek. In fact, being a Geek was the only thing I did well. Other than that, I was pretty mediocre in everything. But somehow, I bought into that myth of turning into a beautiful swan in college. You know, everything would come together and I would find my niche and the women would just want me. Even women like the goddesses of 407. Shit every freshman guy wanted you ladies." Roger took another hit and passed it to Dawn, who looked at Elizabeth to indicate she was taking it with or without her approval. Elizabeth just looked back indicating that that joint better make it to her soon.

"But in college I was just an older mediocre Geek. A Geek who had the misfortune of being assigned a room in Olympia Hall, where the likes of Kip, Larry, Ricky and assorted other bullies thrived on alternating between ignoring or tormenting their inferior peers. And women? Shit. Forget it. And the only thing more pitiful than my social life was my academic record."

Roger paused briefly and looked at each one, trying to sense if they understood everything so far, which they did.

"Well, in March of my freshman year, I had just finished a grueling Psyche 101 mid-term. A mid-term that I knew I failed, but for reasons still unknown, a goddess blessed me with a few extra points, giving me a low D."

Dawn laughed nervously. "E. R. Galah. Yeah, I remember grading that one. You did poorly, which you already knew. But each answer became more and more irreverent and then that quote about mediocrity being such a sin at the end. Well, I went through the test again and I gave you an extra point, here, and an extra point there. Hell, I swear I had never done that before and I never did again," she said reaching out her hand to him.

"It was much appreciated," he said squeezing her hand. "But, even with that test out of the way, I still had to worry about the dreaded Biology 101 mid-term and word in the dorm was that Kip Morgan had gotten his hand on a copy and for the right price, you too could have a copy."

"Oh, my god," Tasha said leaning forward to him, "You were that kid, in the back, that."

"Used to stare at you. You know, the only reason I wanted to do well in that class, was so I could be one of the chosen to help you study or do your lab reports. But, you were smart; you went with the bright students."

"I'm sorry, I swear, I..."

"That's okay Tasha. Actually I take it as a compliment that you didn't recognize me."

"And so you knew about Kip having a much needed copy of an impending test," Elizabeth said getting the gang back on track.

"Sorry, Counselor. There was also a rumor that Kip had gotten his hands on a shit load of pot and again, for the right price, well you know. So, on that Tuesday, I practically depleted my life's savings and early that evening I drove on over the bleachers by the practice field, where Kip had hung his shingle. I was nervous walking across the field, you know, I had no idea what kind of reception Kip would give me. Then I became even more nervous when I heard him laughing with the most beautiful and talented actress on campus."

"What!" Tasha shrieked.

"You were with Kip that evening?" Elizabeth said in shock.

"I was just getting up my nerve to approach them when Miranda came running by," Roger jumped in, anxious to complete the story.

"What?" Now it was Elizabeth and Dawn's turn to shriek.

Roger then completed the whole scenario of Kip's unfortunate demise.

"You mean to tell me, that Miranda has been on the run for two decades because you forgot to tell that story to the police," Elizabeth said in disbelief staring at Tasha.

"I was willing to go to the police. I wanted to," Tasha said in attempt to defend her honor.

"But you didn't, did you?" Elizabeth said viciously.

"She didn't want me to," Tasha cried back at her.

"If you saw the whole thing, why wouldn't she want to you to go to the police?"

"Because Tasha is a lying, cheating, fucking slut," Roger answered.

"Don't call her that," Elisabeth hissed at Roger. "We can call her that, but not you."

"Don't be mad at him, Elizabeth. He is only quoting Miranda, verbatim, I might add. I had no idea you heard."

"I heard everything. I was hiding in the bushes about fifty yards away. Elizabeth, Miranda knew that it would boil down to her and Tasha's words against the words of Larry and Ricky. And Miranda knew that Tasha was not the most credible witness to have on the stand."

"I can attest to that, professionally and personally speaking," Elizabeth said.

"So instead, she made Tasha promise to keep quiet about it. Their original plan was to go back to the dorm and act ignorant. At that point, I began to head back to my car, and Tasha gave Miranda money from Elizabeth's box and the keys to Dawn's car."

"What!" the two of them screamed again.

"And just as I was getting near my car, I heard another car come down the main road and then Ricky's voice shouting out to Kip. And then to Miranda, who by then was running toward Dawn's car. I took off like a bat out of hell, but I tell you, she caught up to me in no time. I looked at her and she looked at me, we didn't know each other, but you know, one social outcast can recognize another. And so I jumped in my car and followed her for

miles.   Eventually we pulled over and she
jumped into my car.   We then drove to some
Norman Bates type motel and I checked in, and
snuck her in.   We sat there for a bit before
getting a bad case of the giggles, which led
us to covering each other's mouth.   Well, that
touch led to more touching, and before we knew
it, we were under the sheets making love.
Grand glorious love.   Which wasn't too bad,
considering we were both virgins?"   Roger
looked down for a few seconds.   "We also
talked.   I mean really talked.   I, for the
first time confessed to somebody, that I
wanted to work on films.   She thought that was
great," he laughed sentimentally.   "And she
also made me promise to keep quiet.   She felt
that the best plan was to wait and let the
vultures become complacent, before totally
ambushing them.   She swore that the time would
reveal itself.   A few days later I drove her
to meet another activist, who drove her out of
state.   Afterwards I came to campus and of
course, left that thing in your bathroom for
you Tasha."

The other two were about to screech again, but Tasha gave them a signal to just deal with it.

Roger took another hit. "Then after I flunked out, I sold the car, bought a motorcycle and then drove to a farm in upstate New York, where Miranda and a movie camera awaited my arrival." Roger then told a beautiful tale of a goddess and her disciple in a symbiotic relationship in which they both developed and protected each other. But after five years, Miranda had felt her job was done, and it was time for the pupil to forge his own path. Roger's career was taking off, forcing him to travel and Miranda was not quite ready to be out in public.

Roger shut his eyes tightly but, still could not stop a tear or two. The other three hadn't a clue what to say, and so wisely, didn't say anything.

"For the next thirteen years, I did nothing but just focus on my career, which led me to California and ironically to PCU for the recruiting films. That is when I heard about Tonya Giordi."

"What about her" Elizabeth asked.

"That she was a journalism student who had tried to crack the Kip/Miranda case but met with all sorts of resistance. So I gave her an anonymous call and told her that if she could be patient, she could have it all. She agreed, and as you see, she got it all."

"And we helped, significantly, I believe," Elizabeth said. "So if you wanted our help, why didn't you just ask us directly?"

"Are you kidding?" he answered. "You're beautiful Elizabeth, but let's face if, you're a bit of a control freak and with Dawn at your side, I knew you two would wrestle control of this project, and both Tasha and myself had too many secrets at risk for that to happen. What I needed was for Tasha to be in charge of this little sidetrip, and..."

"You appealed to my subversive, sneaky, need a thrill nature," she jumped in.

"That's right. But hey, look at the results! Miranda's name is clear, and our secrets have been kept."

"Okay, and now I need to bring up this subject." Elizabeth said gently.

"Why you three were fucked?"

"I prefer the term, seduced," Elizabeth said gently.

"Are you kidding? To be this close to you three and not go for it. Please," he laughed.

"Now, don't take this the wrong way, everyone," Tasha said. "I can understand how Roger got to me, but what I don't get is how Roger got to the Ice Queen and the Earth Maiden."

"Hey!" the other two said.

"Oh, that was Miranda's doing." Roger said. "She talked about you three quite a bit. She loved and admired you more than you'll ever know." He looked at Elizabeth. "Yes, high society, high achieving Elizabeth, attending her reunion as the Outstanding Alumnus. I knew that you knew that that was an award for somewhat who had reached their pinnacle and I knew that was scaring you. Making you ripe for a little sidetrip with a biker."

"So when, you called and invited me for an evening bike ride, I lied about a night with my parents, and met you in the shadow," she purred, leaning in toward him.

"Topped off with a little leather and some restraints." he added.

"And a whip," she said softly with much affection.

"Whoa, this is gross, I don't want to hear anymore," Tasha yelled. My god, the image she had in her head, but what really shook her was the blood rising to Elizabeth face and fire that was in her eyes as she stared at Roger. There was more passion to this woman at this moment than in the last quarter century combined.

"And Dawn," Roger said, although Tasha was not sure she wanted to hear this story. "I knew you always felt like the ugly stepsister to these two."

"Which is why you came on strong with the debonair savior faire dress and demeanor," Dawn said. She then looked at the other two. "I can rarely justify lying, but when Roger invited to me to a Black Tie Museum Exhibit Opening, well I conjured up a teen hotline training session. Sorry."

Tasha looked at the glow and sense of satisfaction that was now on Dawn's face, and realized that damn, it wasn't just her. This guy was good! And ironically, they all had Miranda to thank for it. "Sometimes it takes a goddess to know how to love a goddess," Tasha whispered to herself.

"So, Roger, for three consecutive nights, you enjoyed a goddess," Tasha said.

"Yes, I did. But you know what?"

"You would have given us all up, for another night with Miranda," Dawn guessed.

"Yes. You three are amazing and I worship you, but Miranda is still the one I love."

"Well, maybe when this whole legal issue comes to a final closure." Elizabeth.

"And maybe not," he said with a catch in his voice. "Listen, I do believe that I have created enough discord in your lives."

He leaned over and kissed Dawn's cheek, who bit her lip to keep from crying. He then approached Elizabeth and she, too, fought back the tears. Then he came over to Tasha.

"It was a hell of journey, don't you think," he said.

"Oh, it was just another Elysian sidetrip," she whispered trying in vain not to get too mushy. But in the end, the tears streamed down her face as he kissed her and then departed.

"Come back, Shane, come back," Tasha whispered.

Chapter twenty-seven:

Life Goes On

It was a Herculean effort to reveal the sad strange truth about Kip Morgan's demise, but the consequences for the minor players evolved at record breaking speed.

Larry Davidson, in exchange for immunity, immediately spilled the beans. Detective Anthony Degas, in exchange for a reduced sentence, confirmed all the spilled beans, and John Morgan, through a lot of legal maneuvering received a light sentence. Elizabeth did get satisfaction, though, in

John's resignation from the PCU Board of Trustees and the quiet demise of the Kip Morgan Athletic Scholarship.

George Weybourne, with the help of Dawn, implemented a Teen Peer Counseling Program at his church. Dawn also introduced a similar program at PCU, and eventually at the Social Services. Her skills in management, political lobbying, and fund-raising, astonished everyone, especially Dawn herself, and within time, more and more programs in need of revamping were assigned to her guardianship.

Elizabeth negotiated a swift settlement between the rape victims and PCU. Her self-reward was a cut in workload, a new Harley-Davidson and membership in a riding club. Tasha did wonder about what kind of friends Elizabeth was making and just how friendly these friends were getting, but chose to mind to mind her own business, at least for the time being.

In a wonderful chain of events, Roger signed a contract with Sam Cannon and began directing television episodes that were originally assigned to Jacob Felding. Jacob Felding reduced his number of episodes to spend more time with his guerilla-theatre company, producing and directing ground-breaking, controversial productions. Jacob felt comfortable making this move, because for the first time in years, his income was not as important to the family's well-being. All the publicity surrounding Miranda created new interest in Tasha Felding, the actress and her much loved, thought-to-be-dead soap character. With clout and Elizabeth behind her, Tasha negotiated one hell of a business package that included her triumphed return to the soap, a production company, and a few guaranteed leads in made for TV movies.

The only player who didn't seem to benefit financially and professionally was, ironically, Miranda Taylor herself. Despite the dropped charges and public display of support, Miranda was still nowhere to be seen.

Elizabeth theorized that Miranda would make a grand entrance on the 20th anniversary. Dawn felt that Miranda needed time and space to adjust, and that she would emerge cautiously. But Tasha feared that maybe Miranda had accomplished what she wanted and was now out of their lives for good.

On March 10, Tasha hung around her home and kept a careful watch for any form of communication from Miranda. Elizabeth and Dawn, at their respective offices and homes, kept their cells phone close, in case Tasha had an update for them. By late afternoon, Tasha was ready to throw in the towel and accept the idea that their game was finished.

"Well, there are still several hours left to this day," Dawn reassured the other two during their conference call. "Let's face it, she has a pretty good psychological handle on us, and maybe, she's just teasing us a bit."

"I have to admit, I was hoping she would just show up in the flesh," said Elizabeth.

"I thought of that possibility, but I doubt it. It would almost be too obvious," Tasha said.

"But it would bring it around full circle. I mean, it was twenty years ago that you last spoke to her," Elizabeth reminded her.

"Listen, I don't know if there will be some communication or not, but all we can do is wait until it happens. Listen, if I hear something or receive something, I'll call you, no matter how late," Tasha told them.

They were saying their good byes, when Tasha quickly jumped in, "Ojai in September?"

"Of course, why not?" asked Elizabeth.

"It's just that, oh, I don't know how to explain it, I was just worried that you wouldn't want to go."

"Well," Dawn offered, "there has been a significant change in our perception of twenty years ago and of each other. Sometimes that alters a relationship severely. It may be something we will have to face and deal with."

"Well, I vote for facing it in Ojai," Tasha stated.

"You're so deep, Tasha," Elizabeth laughed. "Remember give us a call when you know something."

While making lunches for the next day, Tasha was seriously worried. It had been years since Miranda delivered the message this late in the day, and that was when Tasha was doing live theatre or was on location. Tasha did toy with the idea that maybe the message might arrive around the time of the actual accident, and then it hit her: "The practice field," she yelled.

Adrenaline, breaking all traffic rules, and the lack of the California Highway Patrol on the roads, enabled her to reach the destination in record time.

Tasha was relieved to see some joggers in the area, but on the other hand, she felt conspicuous just hanging out. She hoped none of them would call security on her. But then, she'd just call Elizabeth who would call President Riley.

She walked over to the new and improved, but still Satyr green bleachers and looked around, not quite sure what she was searching for. Going around to the back of the bleachers, she looked up and recalled Miranda's athletic body flying down beautifully from the top, as if carried by angles only to be followed by Kip's gorgoneion flight to his death.

"Oh my shit," she said aloud. "Excuse me," she yelled nervously at some runner. "Could you come here for a minute? Please."

"Sure ma'am" said some sweet young thing in a Property of PCU Football t-shirt.

"Say sweetie, was that up there yesterday, do you know?" she asked pointing up to the top railing, where someone had taken a knife and carved in *What a long strange trip it's been!*"

"Wow. I don't think so. I was here yesterday and I was doing sit ups right here and I'm sure I would have seen it."

"Thank you," she smiled.

"Guess someone is finishing up their senior project or something. Needed to let off a little steam."

"I think you're right, dear. I think you're right."

The runner took off and Tasha just marveled at that sight for a good twenty minutes. Then without warning, her eyes swelled with tears and her body experienced some slight spasms. It dawned on Tasha that maybe this was the final good-bye. Miranda may had been clever in the past, but never so brazen. And it had been years since she had spoken in the past tense.

Not wanting to cause a scene, Tasha returned to her car and allowed herself a quick cry before addressing her longtime phantom correspondent.

"Miranda," she said speaking through the tears. "I don't want it to end. I know that the past twenty years must have been difficult for you and you deserve the chance to move on. But I'm not ready for total closure, as Dawn would say. I know I'm being selfish, but that is a trait of mine that has never been a big secret."

Tasha put her hands through her hair. "Miranda, I know the annual contacts were to let me know you were safe. And maybe, to have some fun on your part, you know, contacting me, while eluding the authorities. I enjoyed it too. I enjoyed getting away with something. And not only did I know you were safe. But you knew I was safe. No matter where I was, or doing, you found me. You were in my life, watching over me. Never interfering, never passing judgment, and just watching. I liked that. I don't want it to end. I still need your presence. One contact a year. Is that too much to ask?"

Tasha knew Miranda would receive this communiqué, in some strange mystical manner.

And she also knew that as simple as the question was—will the annual contacts end or not?—the simple answer would not be forthcoming for another 365 days.

Fortunately the same fates that had been watching over Miranda and Tasha these past twenty years would also watch over them this coming year, and they would toss some crumbs of adventure down Tasha's way to help keep her amused and occupied until March 10, 1994. But that still didn't make Tasha feel any better at the moment.

She turned on the ignition and before pulling away, glanced over at the bleachers, where she swore she saw a faint shadow of a 5'7" athletic woman stretching before taking off in the other direction.

"Next year. Same Miranda channel. Same Miranda time," Tasha said putting her foot on the gas.

As she drove away, she threw a kiss at the almost out of view runner and sighed, "Fade out."

About the Author

Sirena West is a part of that magical generation that came of age with Hullabaloo, ushered in MTV and has since graduated to Vh-1. She is grounded in reality, but embraces her inner goddess, and seeks others who do the same. Her daily life revolves around husband, children and a business career, but she always makes sure she leaves room for adventure and tantra massages in mythic proportions. A true film aficionado, Ms. West has created and maintains four film-oriented websites and has written three plays that have been staged.